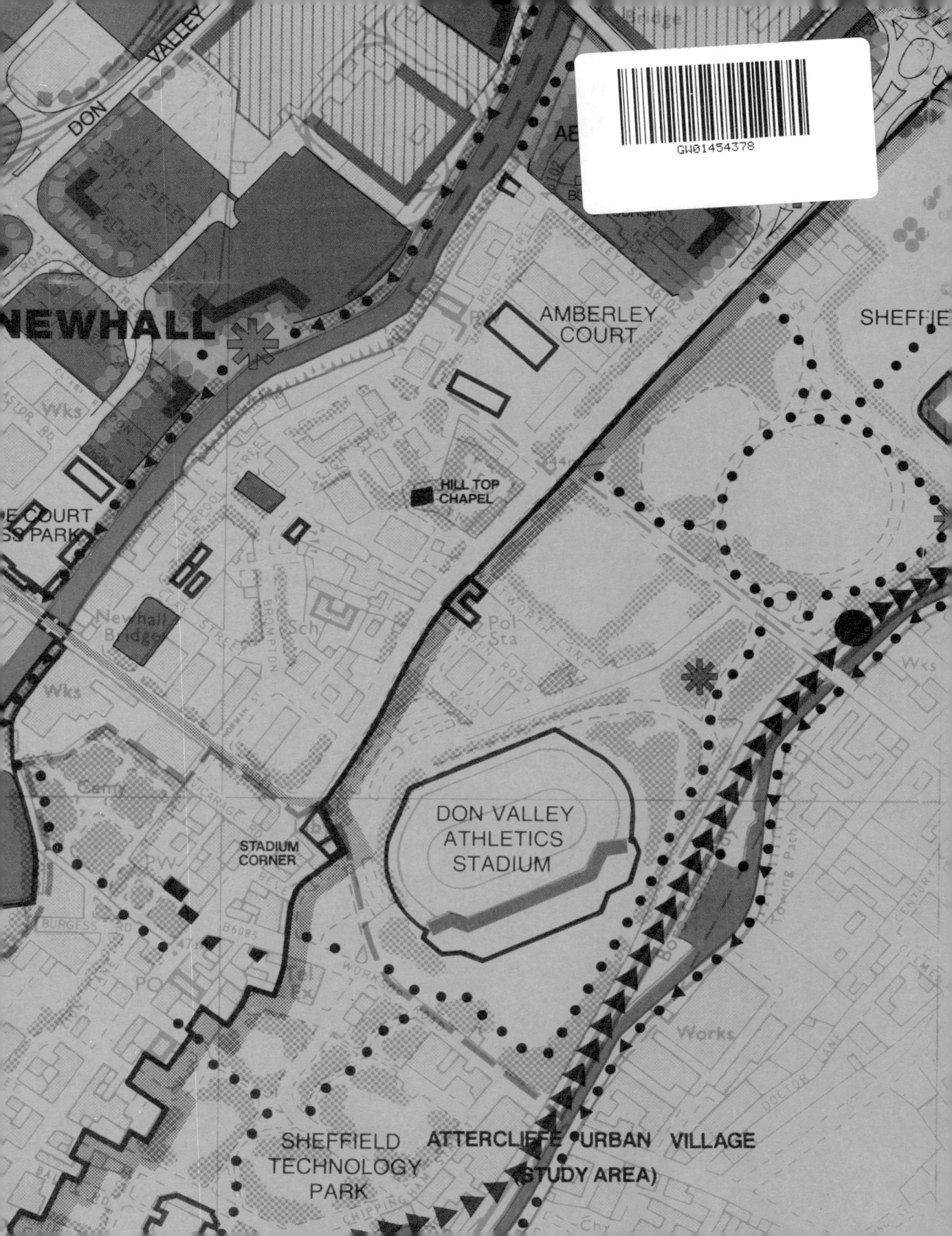

NEWHALL

DON VALLEY

AMBERLEY COURT

SHEFFIE

HILL TOP CHAPEL

Pol Sta

DON VALLEY ATHLETICS STADIUM

STADIUM CORNER

SHEFFIELD TECHNOLOGY PARK

SHEFFIELD ATTERCLIFFE URBAN VILLAGE
(STUDY AREA)

Forging the Valley

FORGING

the VALLEY

David Hey
Martin Olive
Martin Liddament

Sheffield Academic Press

Published by Sheffield Academic Press Ltd
Mansion House
19 Kingfield Road
Sheffield S11 9AS
England

Printed on acid-free paper in Great Britain
by Bookcraft Ltd
Midsomer Norton, Bath

British Library Cataloguing in Publication Data

A catalogue record for this book is available
from the British Library

ISBN 1-85075-647 3

Contents

Foreword

The Lower Don Valley's basic physical features have been formed by the forces of nature and most notably by the River Don itself. The valley bottom constitutes the largest area of flat land in Sheffield and this has been a major influence on its social and economic development.

Over a period of at least some 2500 years the valley has also been shaped by people. This book traces the impact they have had from the earliest iron age fort to the birth of today's space-age, information-based industries.

The theme running through the book is 'change'. For over 2000 years the Lower Don Valley gradually evolved. Change was incremental and would have been barely perceptible to those living in and around it. However, about the middle of the eighteenth century the valley's great industrial period began. At first slowly but then rapidly accelerating until the area became the largest and most important steel producing area in the world.

Virtually all of this growth was unplanned and uncoordinated but nevertheless it brought huge prosperity with it. In the 1980s forces outside the control of those in the Lower Don Valley led to a catastrophic collapse of its industrial base. Dereliction, unemployment and despair became the order of the day. In 1988, the nadir of the Lower Don Valley's fortunes, the Government created the Sheffield Development Corporation and charged it with regenerating the area. During an eight-and-a-half year period a small team of dedicated professionals, numbering no more than about forty at its peak, has led the most rapid and planned period of change the Valley has seen.

Working with numerous public and private partners, this team has succeeded in bringing about the transformation of the Valley. New roads, new buildings, massive environmental improvements and even an airport have certainly changed its physical appearance. However, of more importance, the area's confidence and spirit have been restored. The traditional metal-based industries are thriving, but alongside them now happily sit major new service companies, leisure and retail complexes. The Lower Don Valley is once more a vital and exciting place to be. Those of us who have been privileged to be given the brief opportunity to shape this part of its long history can, I believe, take considerable satisfaction from what has been achieved. It is not often that a small group can contribute so directly, so visibly and so quickly to the regeneration of such an important area.

Hugh Sykes, DL

Notes on Contributors

David Hey is Professor of Local and Family History in the Division of Adult Continuing Education at the University of Sheffield.

Martin Olive is a freelance researcher and writer specializing in the local history of Sheffield and Derbyshire and was previously Local History Librarian at Sheffield City Library.

Martin Liddament is a public relations specialist and was previously Corporate Affairs Manager for the Sheffield Development Corporation.

Illustrations

Illustrations 1 to 45 are drawn from the collection in the Local Studies section of Sheffield Libraries and Information Services. Many of the later photographs come from the library of the Sheffield Development Corporation, and particular acknowledgment should go to Laurance Richardson, John Houlihan and Ian Lawson.

The Early History of the District

David Hey

At first sight, the Lower Don Valley seems an unpromising district to search for evidence of human activity before the profound changes of the nineteenth century, but like most parts of England it has older layers of history which can be carefully peeled away to provide glimpses of an ancient past long before written records begin. The earliest evidence comes from features that remain in the landscape and from place-names, whose interpretation is fraught with difficulties. As we shall see, until well into the eighteenth century the story is about continuity rather than change, the dominant theme of modern times. The Valley had a long, and in many ways an interesting history before its character was utterly transformed by the great steel works of the mid-nineteenth century.

In prehistoric times, the river Don appears to have been a boundary that separated the territories of two British tribes: the Brigantes in the north and the Corieltauvi further south. The earliest surviving evidence of human activity in or near the Lower Don Valley is the remarkably well-preserved Iron Age fort that occupies a commanding position on the top of Wincobank Hill, on the north side of the river. A double rampart and a bank which was constructed of earth over a dry-stone wall surround a 2.5 acre enclosure, whose outline can easily be followed on the ground. Radio-carbon testing of material extracted from the ramparts has given a date of about 500 BC for its construction. It clearly defended a crossing of the river Don and may have been continually occupied until the Romans advanced north in the second half of the first century ad; otherwise, it may have been abandoned, then brought back into use upon the arrival of the Romans on the opposite bank of the river. The presence of such a

Figure 1. Aerial view of Wincobank hill fort. The oval-shaped
enclosure of the Iron Age hill fort (*indicated*) can be picked out
amidst the houses and industrial buildings of the Lower Don Valley.

prominent fort suggests that the district around it was well settled by the Iron Age, but the huge industrial developments of the nineteenth and twentieth centuries have obliterated all other evidence from this early period. The hill fort at Wincobank is a powerful symbol of continuity amidst all the changes that have occurred in the Valley.

The extensive view from the ramparts at Wincobank covers the whole of the Lower Don Valley and stretches far beyond. The view once included the fort that the Romans built for about 800 soldiers at Templeborough, across the river from the Iron Age fort. In his *A Tour through the Whole Island of Great Britain*, published in 1724–26, Daniel Defoe wrote that 'the remains of the Roman fortification or encampment between Sheffield and Rotherham is there still, and very plain to be seen, and, I suppose, may remain so to the end of time'. Its life-span was shorter than Defoe anticipated, however, for in 1916 the steel works of Steel, Peech and Tozer were extended over the site, completely obliterating it. The finds from the excavation are on display in Clifton Park Museum, Rotherham.

The fort was built in three phases, from 54 AD to the late third or perhaps the early fourth century. The example of contemporary forts of a similar size elsewhere in England suggests that a civilian settlement was probably built outside the defences, but no traces of such a settlement have been found. Nor is the Roman name known. The Anglo-Saxons referred to such forts as Brough or Burgh, and as late as 1771 Thomas Jeffreys's map of Yorkshire marked the site as Brough Hill. The prefix Temple- was not recorded before 1559. It seems to have been merely an antiquarian fancy. Roman Templeborough must have been connected by military roads to other forts, notably Castleford, Doncaster, Chesterfield and Brough (near Hope), but few remains of such routes have been discovered. The road from the south-west gate probably followed the Lower Don Valley in a westerly direction until it joined the military road from Lincoln, which came via Littleborough (Notts.), across the river Idle at Bawtry and the river Rother at Catcliffe, and proceeded along Cricket Inn Lane to Sheffield, Stanage and Brough. Templeborough was abandoned upon the withdrawal of the Romans in the early fifth century, and Rotherham and Sheffield gradually became the new focal points of settlement, where the rivers Rother and Sheaf flowed into the Don.

Our third piece of landscape evidence from the remote past is the earthwork now known as the 'Roman Rig', which runs parallel to the Don on the hills to the north of the river, passing close to the fort at Wincobank. Despite its name, it is not thought to be Roman, but to date from sometime after the Roman withdrawal. It was described in 1693 as 'a cussen Dich there called Kempe Ditch'. 'Cussen' is an archaic dialect word meaning cast-up, and 'kemp' means warrior. Daniel Defoe wrote,

> Here is also the famous bank or trench which some call Devil's Bank, others Danes Bank; but 'tis frequent with us to give the honour of such great trenches, which they think was never worth the while for men to dig, to the devil, as if he had more leisure, or that it was less trouble to him than to a whole army of men. This bank, 'tis said, runs five miles in length; in some places 'tis called Kemp Bank, in others Temple's Bank.

Despite the fact that some stretches of this earthwork have been excavated, we are not much wiser about its date or purpose. Several sections of the ditch survive, especially near Wentworth and Swinton, but they are not as prominent as they were in Defoe's time. The 'Roman Rig' is longer than Defoe thought, for it runs ten miles from Sheffield in the west, via Wincobank, to the marshy ground near Mexborough and Kilnhurst in the east. The southern bank of the ditch was not solidly constructed, but merely thrown up. It seems likely that the earthwork was not intended to be defensive, but marked a frontier, just north of the river Don.

Our first documentary evidence for settlement in and around the Lower Don Valley comes from the Domesday Book of 1086, but this record is tantalisingly brief and enigmatic. Sheffield, Attercliffe, Tinsley and Rotherham are all recorded, as is a small manor called Grimeshou, which was probably associated with Grimesthorpe. Sheffield and Attercliffe formed part of the much larger territory known as Hallamshire, which was defined in later times as the parish of Sheffield, the parish of Ecclesfield and the chapelry of Bradfield. Tinsley was a small manor and a chapel–of–ease within the parish of Rotherham. Other neighbouring settlements were probably also in existence by the eleventh century (and possibly long before), but as the Domesday Book was concerned only with manors the names of these minor places were not recorded until the thirteenth century, when local records became fuller.

Sheffield and Rotherham were named after their rivers. Attercliffe has been thought to mean 'at the cliff', but the first part of the name is more likely to have been derived from a shortened version of an Old English personal name such as Aethelred. The cliff was levelled in Victorian times when the river was diverted and Sanderson's steel works was built on the site, but it was shown as a prominent feature of the landscape in a view of Christ Church, the new Anglican church of the 1820s. J.M. Wilson's *Imperial Gazetteer of England and Wales* (1870) noted the 'abrupt precipice' overhanging the Don which was thought to have given Attercliffe its name.

Grimeshou probably took its name from the burial mound of someone with the Old Norse personal name Grimr, whose 'outlying farmstead' became known as Grimesthorpe; the two neighbouring farms at Osgathorpe and Skinnerthorpe were named after other early settlers. The place-name evidence suggests that the burial mounds of the leading inhabitants of the district must once have been prominent features of the local landscape, for Tinsley's name is derived from the burial mound of someone with the Old English personal

Figure 2. Christ Church, Attercliffe. A mid-nineteenth-century view of the new church, showing the cliff that gave Attercliffe its name.

name Tynni, and Wincobank, which was known simply as Wincoe or Winkowe until the late sixteenth century, refers to the burial mound of someone with another Old English personal name. Meadow Hall (which was on the hill on the other side of the Blackburn valley from the present shopping centre, and on the line of the 'Roman Rig') was recorded as Madhou in 1300. This name, too, refers to a burial mound; the first part may be a personal name, though it could be 'maiden'. All signs of these burial mounds have long been obliterated. Only their ancient names have remained.

Other place-names that were first recorded in the thirteenth century, but which are probably older, include Darnall ('secluded land in a nook on a boundary'), Staniforth (a lost place-name near Wincobank meaning 'stony ford', and the source of a local surname), and Carbrook ('the stream in the marsh'). The first element in Carbrook's name is the same as the last element in the Wicker, which is reasonably interpreted as 'the marsh where willow trees grew'. The name Brightside did not appear until the sixteenth century and seems to have been an attempt to make sense of an older name Brekesherth, which was recorded with a variety of spellings from the twelfth century onwards until it disappeared about the time that the form Brightside came into use. This older name appears to combine 'hearth' with an Old English personal name.

The Lower Don Valley had some administrative unity in the Middle Ages and later centuries. When Sheffield was made a borough in 1843 and a city fifty years later, the area that came under its jurisdiction was exactly that of the mediaeval parish, which covered 22,370 acres, stretching from Stanage Pole in the west to Carbrook in the east. Before the creation of the borough, this enormous parish was divided into six townships for local government purposes. The most easterly, and smallest, of these was Attercliffe township, or the Township of Attercliffe-cum-Darnall to give it its full title. The township was 1336 acres in extent and, as can be seen from William Fairbank's map of the parish in 1795, it covered most of the district that in 1988 came under the authority of the Sheffield

Development Corporation. Its northern border was the river Don, its western boundary was the ditch and wall that surrounded the mediaeval deer park of the lords of Sheffield Castle (commemorated in such names as Park Hill and the Manor, and by the Nunnery, which has no known connection with a religious site and therefore probably had the alternative meaning of a brothel), to the south lay the parish of Handsworth, and to the east the manor and chapelry of Tinsley.

The village of Attercliffe was the focal point of the Lower Don Valley. Most of its houses and cottages were either arranged around the triangular Attercliffe Green (which was known as Goose Turd Green in 1637) or they were strung out along the road from Sheffield to Rotherham. The regularity of the property arrangements around the green suggests a deliberate planned rebuilding of the settlement at some unknown period in the past. Many English villages, particularly in the North, were re-built on new sites both before and after the Norman Conquest, but we cannot date such

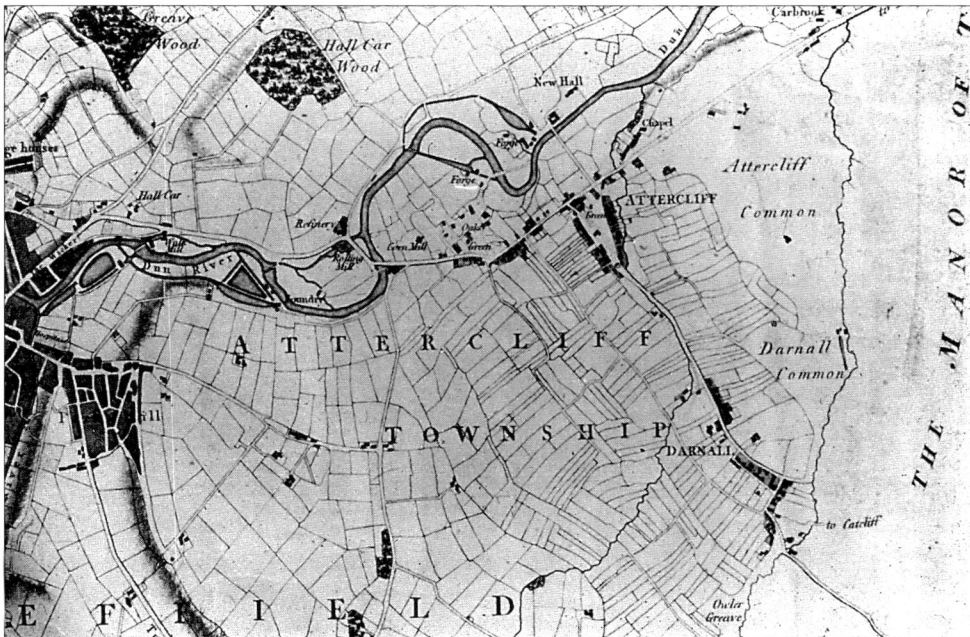

Figure 3. William Fairbank's map of the parish of Sheffield, 1795 (detail). The common pastures and the strips of the open-fields have not yet been enclosed. Attercliffe village is arranged around its green and strung out along the road from Sheffield.

events precisely, for few places have adequate records before the thirteenth century. Darnall seems to have experienced similar re-building, for a survey by John Harrison in 1637 refers to the southern tip of the township, in the fields just beyond Sheffield Park wall, as 'Old Town', a border position that confirms the meaning of Darnall's name. We may speculate that the village was moved to a new site on the Attercliffe to Handsworth road at the same time as Attercliffe Green was established. After these dramatic changes, the plans of the two villages remained unchanged for centuries.

The inhabitants of Attercliffe farmed their arable land in three large open-fields which were divided into strips. The 1795 map shows that this pattern remained largely intact from the Middle Ages until the rearrangements that were made under the Attercliffe Enclosure Act of 1810, culminating in the Award of 1820. The low-lying land between the Sheffield–Rotherham road and the river Don was used as meadows, except where Beighton Green (named after a local family and known later as Oaks Green, after another family) stretched from the road towards Attercliffe Forge. The three open-fields, where cereals were grown, were known as Crossgate, Dean and Park Fields. Crossgate Field took its name from a track known as Crossgate Way, which served as a back lane that separated the crofts of the farmhouses and cottages of the village from the strips of the open-fields, both in Attercliffe and in Darnall. It still exists as a route, under the name of Shirland Lane. Dean Field lay to the south and Park Field stretched from Pinfold Lane (the modern Staniforth Road) as far as the boundary of Sheffield Park.

Each of Attercliffe's three fields was divided into blocks of strips known as flatts or furlongs. Originally, these fields were farmed to a plan agreed at the manorial court, but the survey of 1637 shows that by then many strips had been combined and perhaps had already been taken out of the communal system of farming. They varied in size from 0.25 to 1.25 acres. Darnall had its separate three-field system. The 1795 map shows that the patterns of the fields were different on either side of the tiny brook which divided Darnall from Attercliffe. Both sets of fields were grazed in common after the harvest. The two villages also had large common pastures in the eastern part of the township, bordering on Tinsley. By 1810 about 239 acres of commons and 50 acres of strips remained to be enclosed into new fields. The township of Attercliffe-cum-Darnall was the last part of Sheffield parish to be enclosed, presumably because the lord of Hallamshire did not own large blocks of land there and considerable amounts were held by freeholders.

The township of Attercliffe-cum-Darnall had the flattest farm land in the parish of Sheffield. Farming here was carried on in a similar manner to agriculture in the Vale of York or the Midland Plain. The system was very different from that practised by the sheep and cattle farmers on the western side of Sheffield, and from that of their immediate neighbours. To the east, much of Tinsley was enclosed within the deer park of its mediaeval lord. Like the parks at Ecclesall and Shirecliffe, by the sixteenth or the seventeenth centuries Tinsley Park had been converted into coppice woodland. The name is now associated with a steel works and a golf course, but a remnant of the old wood and the mediaeval boundary ditch still mark the southern edge of the park. North of the river Don lay another of the six townships of the old parish of Sheffield, that which was known as Brightside Bierlow. (Bierlow was an Old Norse word for a township and was also used for Ecclesall Bierlow.) Here the fields were irregular-shaped pastures and meadows rather than strips of arable, and the hillsides were covered by several old coppice or 'spring' woods, which were carefully managed in order to provide charcoal, pit props, fencing, hurdles and so on. Thus, a survey of 1642 reported that the woods at Wincoe and Hall Carr had not been felled for 24 years, that Burngreave was 'now felling for punch wood' (that is for pit props), and that Wilkinson Springwood and Cook Wood had been cut down for similar and other uses during the past three years. In contrast, neither Attercliffe nor Darnall had any woods at all. Today, only Wincobank Wood survives from the group of coppice woods that were marked on William Fairbank's map of Sheffield parish in 1795.

Most farms in the Lower Don Valley were small. The farmers depended on their right to graze a few animals on the commons, and most of them had another occupation, particularly that of cutler or scissorsmith. This dual occupation of the farmer-craftsman was the normal way of life for families in many parts of England during the sixteenth, seventeenth and eighteenth centuries and probably had been in previous centuries before adequate records began to be kept. The inventories of personal estate that were attached to the wills of this period commonly show that Attercliffe cutlers and scissorsmiths had a cow or two, a small flock of sheep, some corn and hay, and a manure stack. For example, John Bullas, a cutler who died in 1696, had oats, straw and hay in his barn, together with a mare, a cow, a pig, and some winter-sown corn, but very little farm equipment other than some troughs and a wheelbarrow. In his smithy he had a pair of bellows and a stithy (anvil), four vices, six hammers, a trough, a glazer, four saws, tongs, files and other cutlers' tools, some iron, steel and wire, and some finished knives and blades. John Green, a cutler who died in 1716, had two pair of bellows, stithies, stocks and coultroughs, a vice, nine hammers, a glazer and tongs in his smithy, and a stone, three axletrees, a glazer, two bands, a wheel chimney and some 'other gears' at a grinding wheel. He also had a cow, some oat seed, and manure, but no equipment other than a sled. John Shemeld, a scissorsmith who died in 1752, had a few simple tools and equipment in his smithy and at the grinding wheel, and ten sheep, a cow, hay and straw, and 'manure in the fold'.

This small scale of enterprise had long been typical of the way of life of the many cutlers and scissorsmiths in Attercliffe township and in Wincobank. They were a distinctive group amongst the numerous cutlers of Hallamshire, who by the sixteenth century had triumphed over their provincial rivals, such as the cutlers of Thaxted and Salisbury, until their reputation was inferior only to the craftsmen of London. Hallamshire men have been making cutlery for at least 700 years and were probably doing so in earlier centuries before written records began. Originally, the trade was organized through the manorial court of the lord of Sheffield castle.

The mighty Earls of Shrewsbury gave their powerful support to the growth of the local trade, and the district had the inestimable advantage of numerous sites on its fast-flowing rivers for grinding wheels and the perfect sandstone for grinding, advantages that its rivals lacked. By the sixteenth century, when a national commentator observed that Hallamshire had many smiths and cutlers, the local iron was considered inadequate for the cutting edges that were required, so iron was imported all the way from north Spain. By that time, Hallamshire's natural resources and long tradition of skilled craftsmanship allowed the local trade to absorb transport costs when selling its products in competition with its rivals. By the eighteenth century, the district had triumphed even over London.

The death of Gilbert Talbot, the last of the Earls of Shrewsbury to live for part of each year in Sheffield, and the passing of the Hallamshire estates to the absentee Dukes of Norfolk, forced the cutlers to found their own organisation to oversee the cutlery trade. Numerous men from the eastern parts of Sheffield parish joined the Cutlers' Company when it was incorporated in 1624. They included Robert Carr of Attercliffe, who was an Assistant in the first Company in 1624–25 and Master Cutler in 1639. His son Stephen served as Master Cutler in 1660. The trade continued to grow in the second half of the seventeenth century. When a government tax was levied on domestic and industrial hearths in 1672, one in every three houses in the township of Attercliffe-cum-Darnall had a smithy attached. Only the centre of Sheffield had a higher concentration of smithies at that time. The east end of Sheffield parish was already semi-industrial in character and was very different from the western parts of the parish and from other rural districts within Hallamshire. The units of production were very small by modern standards, of course, but few seventeenth-century English villages were as industrialized in the sense that so many of the inhabitants were engaged in manufacturing as was Attercliffe. The Lower Don Valley had begun to acquire a special character of its own.

During the seventeenth century the source of supply of the foreign iron that was used for the best-quality cutting edges in and around Sheffield changed from northern Spain to the Rhine and then to Sweden. The first steel works in south Yorkshire had been built by Charles Tooker of Rotherham, by 1642, but the local steel industry remained small until well into the eighteenth century. The south Yorkshire iron industry was far more ancient. Production methods had been revolutionized when George, the sixth Earl of Shrewsbury and lord of Hallamshire, had built the first charcoal blast furnaces and associated forges in south Yorkshire. Starting during the winter of 1573–74, he had brought workmen of French nationality or descent from the Weald of Sussex and Kent to build ironworks on his estates at Attercliffe, Kimberworth and Wadsley. The Upper and Nether Hammers (or Sheffield and Attercliffe Forges as they were alternatively known) were in production by 1581. The Upper Hammer on the south side of the river Don was the smaller of the two; in 1587 it forged 84 tons of iron. The Nether Hammer on the north side of the river converted 144 tons of pig iron from the earl's furnaces at Kimberworth and Wadsley. Some of this iron was used to make frying pans and dripping pans. In retrospect, we can see that the Upper and Nether Hammers were the forerunners of the iron and steel works that were eventually to transform the character of the lower Don valley, but nobody in the sixteenth century could have predicted such changes.

The distinctive surnames of some of the immigrants who operated the forges and furnaces in this period enable us to identify their ancestors amongst the 'aliens' who had come from Lorraine and other parts of northern France to work in Sussex and Kent from the 1520s onwards. Thus, the Vintins were in south-eastern England from at least the 1540s before they migrated north. William Vintin was married at Sheffield Parish Church (now the Cathedral) in 1611. He and his descendants were millwrights or carpenters at Attercliffe Forge, the men who installed the huge tilt hammers and who saw to the smooth running of the operation. In 1659 Peter Vintin of Attercliffe Forge married Anne Tullett, the descendant of another French immigrant. William Perigoe of Attercliffe Forge, whose marriage was recorded at Sheffield in 1637, came from a similar

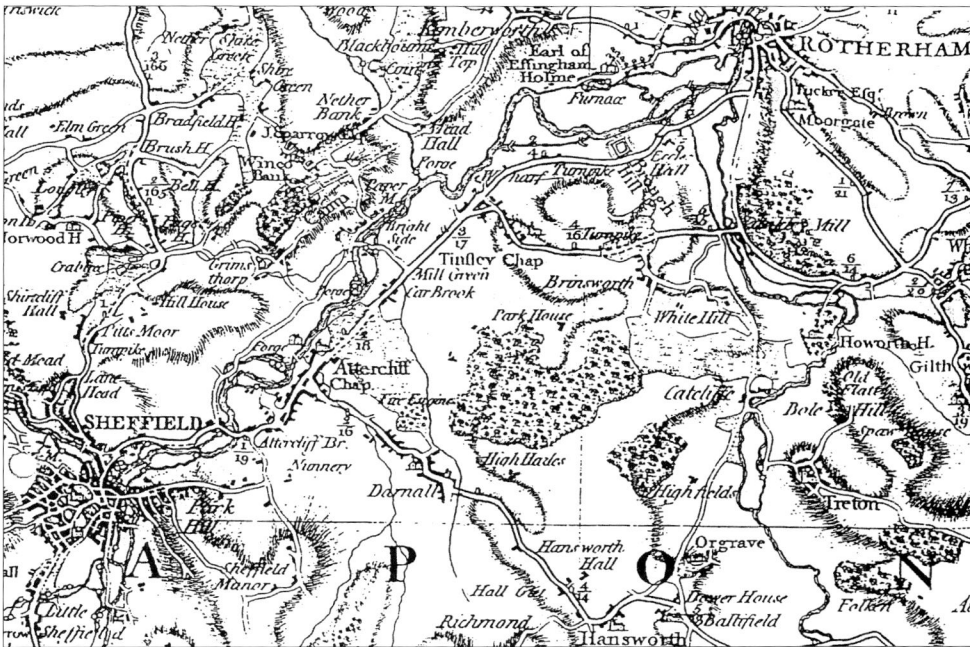

Figure 4. Thomas Jeffreys' map of Yorkshire, 1767–72 (detail). The map shows the Lower Don Valley before the enormous changes of the nineteenth century. Many place-names can be recognized. Some industries had already been established by the river.

background. So did David and John Hussey, frying pan makers of Attercliffe Forge in the mid-seventeenth century, and Roland Huse, whose son and namesake was baptized at Sheffield in 1646. The Tylers, Jordans, Bartholomews and Gillams may have arrived by the same route, but we cannot be certain in these cases for similar surnames had been established in Hallamshire in earlier times. Some of the immigrants did not stay long, but others, like the Vintins and the Husseys, became absorbed in local society. People with these surnames who are listed in the current Sheffield telephone directory may well be descendants of these foreign ironworkers.

The arrival of these immigrants must have caused quite a stir, for most of the local families had long been resident in and around Hallamshire. It is clear from a study of the parish register, wills, and the Cutlers' Company records that the township of Attercliffe-cum-Darnall contained a large group of families which stayed in the same place over a long period of time. Some of these bore surnames such as Staniforth, Dungworth, Beighton, Brewell (from Braithwell) and Bullas (from Bullhouse), which had been derived from south Yorkshire settlements. Other names, such as Scargill, had been well known in south-west Yorkshire since the fourteenth century. Even families with common surnames such as Green, Hibbert, Allen or Carr can be traced through several generations in Attercliffe. These core families, of course, were often connected by marriage. Other links were forged when a boy served an apprenticeship with a neighbouring master, mostly with cutlers and scissorsmiths, but sometimes with maltsters, carpenters, and others. The members of these long-resident families were the ones who filled the local offices of constable, overseer of the poor, and churchwarden, and who preserved local traditions and ensured continuity. Other people came and went and appear only fleetingly in the records, but this core group which stayed put over the generations ensured that a real sense of community existed in the eastern part of Sheffield parish during the sixteenth, seventeenth and eighteenth centuries.

Until well into the seventeenth century the inhabitants of the Lower Don Valley lived in houses that were timber-framed and roofed with thatch. A survey of properties in Sheffield parish that belonged to the Church Burgesses, made in 1616 and updated in 1672, noted that George Gill had a house on Attercliffe Green that was slated, together with a thatched house at the back. His neighbour, William Setchfield, occupied a house, smithy and barn, all of which were thatched. Nearby, Rose Smyth, a widow, rented a slated house and a little thatched house, and Edmond Swift rented '15 Bay of houses and 3 outshutts all Thatcht saveing halfe a Bay'.

The inventories of personal estate that were attached to local wills from the late seventeenth to the late eighteenth centuries show that the main living room was called the 'house' and that the adjoining downstairs 'parlour' long remained the best bedroom. The upstairs 'chambers' were, at first, used as bedrooms for children and servants or as workrooms and storage space. The service room on the ground floor was either a 'kitchen' or a 'buttery'. Thus, in 1707 the rooms of Thomas Marriott, scissorsmith, were listed as house, parlour, buttery, chambers, smithy and barn, and in 1737 Abijah Oakes, scissorsmith, had a house, two parlours, a brewhouse and cellar, and a house chamber, middle chamber, and lumber chamber upstairs. Many more such examples could be given. As in other parts of England at that time, the standard arrangement was to have three rooms in a line on the ground floor, with

Figure 5. 'The Old House at Washford Bridge', drawn by William Topham, c.1882.

chambers above. Extra rooms were sometimes added in the form of lean-tos or outshutts. A house built by Elizabeth Roades at Washford Bridge, in 1671, was a substantial example of this type.

The gentry, of course, had superior accommodation. When William Burton of Royds Mill died in 1720, his rooms were described as hall, best dining room, kitchen, brewhouse, bolting house (for baking), garden house, parlour, little dining room, cellar, chamber over the pantry, green chamber, nursery, far garret, garret, corn chamber and barn. Less grand were the rooms of the house belonging to William Hoole, gentleman, of Tinsley, which were listed in 1738 as hall, kitchen, brewhouse, pantry, old parlour, kitchen chamber, bed chamber, chamber over the old parlour, and various outbuildings.

The gentry led the way in building houses of stone instead of wood. The old Carbrook Hall was a timber-framed structure, but when Stephen Bright (1583–1642) inherited the property he built a new wing in stone on the west side of the old house. An iron fireback, inscribed 'SB 1623',

Figure 6. Carbrook Hall. This drawing by Edward Blore, published in Joseph Hunter's *Hallamshire* in 1819, shows the original timber-framed house and Stephen Bright's new stone wing of 1623.

dates this extension. Stephen Bright was bailiff of Hallamshire and lord of Ecclesall, and thus the most important resident in the parish of Sheffield at that time. He received a grant of arms just before his death in 1642. The new wing was used as a parlour block and was clearly intended to impress people with the high quality of its work. Bright used craftsmen who had worked for the Earls of Shrewsbury and the Earls of Devonshire at Sheffield Manor Lodge, Chatsworth and Hardwick, men who could plaster ceilings and walls with elaborate strapwork designs and naturalistic foliage. Wooden panelling and a carved oak fireplace surround completed the splendid interior. The original timber-framed house was demolished in the 1840s, but the new parlour block survives intact, together with a later seventeenth-century wing and a central linking block of the 1840s. The alterations were finished by 1852 when Carbrook Hall Estate (consisting of the building and 116 acres of land) was put up for sale. The seventeenth-century interior can be inspected readily, for Carbrook Hall is now a pub. It is easily the finest surviving building in the valley from the period before the great industrial changes of the nineteenth century.

Stephen Bright's son, Sir John Bright, eventually left Carbrook for Badsworth, five miles south of Pontefract. The other prominent gentry family in the eastern part of Sheffield parish were the Spencers of

Figure 7. Carbrook Hall plasterwork. The plasterwork is of a style that was popular amongst the gentry of the Sheffield district in the early seventeenth century.

Attercliffe Hall. Their house was largely dismantled in 1868, the rest being demolished in 1934. William Spencer the younger (1584–1649), who inherited the property in 1622, was responsible for the rebuilding. Old photographs show that it, too, had a fine display of plasterwork, particularly in the upper chamber. The plasterwork panel which was above the fireplace now adorns Cartledge Hall, near Holmesfield (Derbyshire). It expressed the puritan sentiment that: 'What soever thou dost take in hande thinke of the ende and seldom so shalt thou offend'. William Spencer was also lord of Darnall and the owner of Bramley Grange, where he built a house similar to that of his friend Stephen Bright of Carbrook. The status of the family is suggested by a bequest in his son's will in 1684 of 'my gold ring with my coat of arms engraved thereon'. The main downstairs rooms of Attercliffe Hall were described upon the death of the younger William Spencer in 1686 as hall, dining parlour and little parlour. He also had a study with £50 worth of books. The service rooms consisted of a kitchen, brewhouse, bolting house, buttery, pantry, cellar, starch house and milk house. The various upstairs chambers included one for the maids. Spencer's farm stock comprised three bulls, eleven cows and heifers, four calves, eight horses and mares, one foal, four pigs and twelve sheep. He had twelve acres of barley, 12.5 acres of wheat and rye, fourteen acres of oats, and a considerable store of hay. He also had oats, wheat and rye in two corn chambers, and various items of farming equipment in his barn and malt house. Stacks of manure, lime and coal stood in and around the farmyard. The rural image that is conjured up by this inventory is similar to that depicted in the surviving drawing of Carbrook Hall.

The Brights and the Spencers were prominent puritans in the first half of the seventeenth century and the leading Nonconformist families after the Restoration of King Charles II in 1660. Stephen Bright's son, Sir John Bright of Carbrook Hall, had been a colonel in the Parliamentary army and governor of Sheffield Castle during the Civil War, MP for the West Riding in 1654–55, and High Sheriff of Yorkshire. He was made a baronet upon the Restoration, but he refused to conform to the Church of England and patronized Nonconformist ministers who had been ejected from their livings. William Spencer, junior, had been educated at Cambridge University and Gray's Inn before serving as a lieutenant-colonel in the Parliamentary army and subsequently as a Justice of the Peace.

Stephen Bright and William Spencer the elder had been responsible for the rebuilding of the mediaeval chapel-of-ease which served Attercliffe and Brightside townships, just as Ecclesall Chapel provided for the inhabitants of the western parts of Sheffield parish. The early history of Attercliffe Chapel is obscure, but it is known to have stood on Beighton Green and

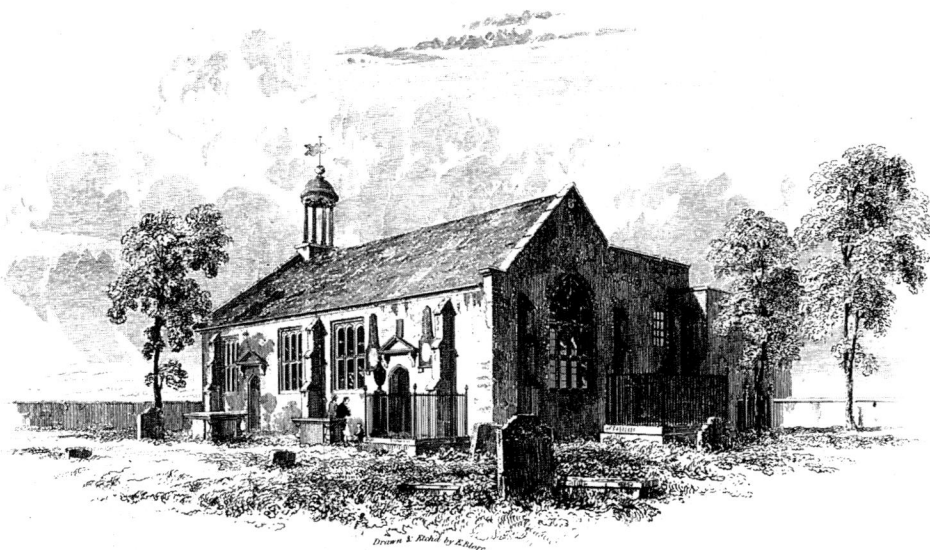

Figure 8. Hill Top Chapel, Attercliffe. Edward Blore's drawing shows the chapel
before it was reduced to its present size.

to have been converted into two dwellings after its dissolution under the terms of the Chantries Act (1547). The new chapel that was built at Hill Top between 1629 and 1636 reflected the puritan beliefs of Stephen Bright and William Spencer in the austerity of its design. The building (which was remodelled in 1909) is a plain oblong with windows still entirely in the Gothic tradition and an open timber roof.

Upon the Restoration of Charles II in 1660, the puritans were forced on the defensive. Matthew Bloome, the assistant minister at Sheffield Parish Church who took the services at Attercliffe Chapel, was one of those clergymen who were ejected from their livings in 1662 because they refused to conform to the practices of the Church of England. Bloome continued to preach in his own house at Attercliffe, then after spending some time in York prison for this defiance he moved to Shirecliffe Hall. The gentry halls at Carbrook, Attercliffe and Shirecliffe remained centres of religious dissent during the reigns of Charles II and James II. Nonconformist meeting houses were registered at Attercliffe during brief periods of toleration in 1669 and 1672–73 before the Glorious Revolution of 1688 swept away the restrictions.

Figure 9. The Reverend Timothy Jollie, Pastor of the Sheffield Independent Congregation and Master of the Attercliffe Academy.

In 1686, the year that both Matthew Bloome and William Spencer died, the Rev. Richard Frankland took a lease of Attercliffe Hall and turned it into a Nonconformist Academy for teaching the sons of Dissenters and for training boys who wished to enter the ministry. Frankland's Academy had been founded twelve years earlier at Rathmell in north-west Yorkshire and had already moved three times. In July 1689, after the Toleration Act finally allowed Nonconformist congregations to meet openly, Frankland returned to Rathmell, but in 1691 the Rev. Timothy Jollie, a former Frankland scholar and now the pastor of the Sheffield Independent Congregation, refounded the Attercliffe Academy. By 1700 he had trained 40 ministers as well as other boys. Such academies gained a high reputation over a wide area and even attracted the sons of men who conformed to the Church of England. Attercliffe was one of the best-known academies in the country. Amongst its famous pupils were Thomas Secker (a future Archbishop of Canterbury), John Bowes (Lord Chancellor of Ireland), Nicholas Sanderson (the blind Thurlstone boy who became Professor of Mathematics at Cambridge) and Dr John Evans (a leading London Nonconformist). Poor boys were sometimes enabled to study there without the payment of fees. After Jollie's death in 1714 the academy was continued by his successor, the Rev. John Wadsworth, until about 1740. Meanwhile, the dissenting congregation at Attercliffe had continued to flourish. It was at its peak during the ministry of the Rev. Samuel Blythe of Norton Lees and numbered 250 in 1715, but then it gradually lost support and was dissolved in 1750.

Some of the 250 members of the congregation came from beyond the Lower Don Valley. It is difficult to obtain precise figures for the population of the Township of Attercliffe-cum-Darnall before the first national census of 1801. A secondary source claims that the township had 240 inhabitants in 1616 (when Sheffield township had 2207), but as the original document does not survive we must treat this information cautiously. The hearth tax return of 1672 listed 123 householders, 22 of whom (17.9 per cent) were poor people who were exempted from payment. The proportion of poor people is rather low, judging by what we know of other contemporary communities, so perhaps the numbers should be adjusted. In two later counts of the population, the average household in Attercliffe contained 4.4 persons (in 1736) and 4.7 people (in 1782). We might therefore conclude that in 1672 the population of Attercliffe-cum-Darnall was about 600. As in other parts of the country, this figure was soon to rise considerably. By 1736 the population of the township was 1075 and by 1801 it had reached 2281. Much of this rise was due to earlier marriages and thus slightly larger families, some of it to lower death rates, and some to immigration. The migrants did not travel very far. Most marriage partners were found from within Hallamshire or from just beyond, and most of the apprentices to the cutlery trades came from no further than twenty miles or so. The 'Attercliffe township book', which notes the names of poor immigrants whom it was feared might become a burden on the poor rates, shows that in the first half of the eighteenth century most of these immigrants travelled only a few miles and that very few came from beyond the West Riding of Yorkshire or Derbyshire. Nevertheless, the growth of the population must have excited much local comment at the time. It was clear that changes were occurring more rapidly than ever before.

The main road through the Lower Don Valley was that which left Sheffield via Lady's Bridge and the Wicker. It kept to the north bank of the river until it entered Attercliffe township at Washford Bridge. The old crossing had originally consisted of a series of stepping stones, known as 'the west ford'. The earliest reference to a bridge on this site is from 1535, when George Moore left a bequest in his will to 'Westforth Bridge'. As 'west' sounds like 'wesh' and as 'wesh' and 'wash' are interchangeable in local dialect, by 1607 the name was sometimes written as 'Washford Bridge'. In 1647 it was referred to as 'Westforth alias Attercliffe Bridge'. The old wooden bridge was taken down in 1672 and replaced by a stone one. In 1752 this bridge was said to be 'of good hewn stone' and to be 92 feet 6 inches long and 13 feet wide. It was one of the bridges that were maintained out of county rather than parish rates, for it was on a busy highway. The road continued through Attercliffe and Carbrook to Tinsley, where it divided, one branch continuing to Rotherham and Doncaster, and the other turning south-east to the inland port of Bawtry.

Figure 10. Washford Bridge. David Martin's view of 1791 shows the bridge that had recently replaced the one built in 1672. It, too, was soon to be replaced. The windmill was on Windmill Lane, near the later Firth Park. The outline of Wincobank Hill is exaggerated for artistic effect.

Water transport was much cheaper than land transport, especially for heavy, bulky goods, such as those made of iron and steel. Until the middle years of the eighteenth century, many of the products of Hallamshire were carried to Bawtry, where they were placed in barges and taken along the river Idle to Stockwith; there they were transferred to larger vessels and sent down the river Trent to Hull, the east coast ports, and to London. The Cutlers' Company spent much time and energy in supporting a scheme to make the river Don navigable, so that the expensive journey overland to Bawtry could be avoided. Early attempts failed because of the opposition of the Duke of Norfolk, who feared that his ironworks and cutlers' grinding wheels on the river below Sheffield would be harmed by having their supply of water cut off. A compromise was finally agreed in 1726–27, when two Acts of Parliament authorized Doncaster Corporation to improve the navigability of the river as far inland as Doncaster and the Cutlers' Company to make the river navigable as far as Tinsley, on the eastern boundary of Hallamshire. A 'River Dun Navigation Company' was formed, and by 1740 the work had been completed as far as Rotherham. Eleven years later, the project was finished with the opening of a new wharf at Tinsley, not far from the junction of the two roads from Doncaster and Bawtry. The commercial importance of the river navigation was enormous, for transport costs were cut dramatically.

Yet, another 68 years passed before the opposition of the Duke of Norfolk could be overcome and the navigation extended westwards to the Canal Basin in Sheffield.

The 'River Dun Navigation Company' was given responsibility for improving and maintaining the road that continued west to Sheffield from the wharf at Tinsley. The Company made some improvements to this road in 1758, but they tackled the job without enthusiasm. Meanwhile, the leading landowners and businessmen of south Yorkshire had begun to take a serious interest in improving the major local roads by obtaining Acts of Parliament which allowed them to set up turnpike trusts. These trusts were empowered to charge tolls, which went towards the expenses of maintaining the roads. The local roads which were turnpiked during the eighteenth century were ancient highways, for the object of turnpiking was simply to improve existing routes. The earliest turnpike road in south-west Yorkshire was the highway which came over the moors from Woodhead to the Don Navigation at Rotherham and Doncaster, a route that was improved in

Figure 11. The locks at Tinsley. This view of c.1905 shows boats that have come up the Don Navigation from Fishlake to the toll house (in the background).

1741. The southern road from Sheffield, via Chesterfield and Derby to London, was turnpiked in 1756 and the northern and western routes to Leeds and Manchester were turnpiked two years later. Attention was then turned to the Lower Don Valley. In 1760 a turnpike trust was created to improve the continuation of the Sheffield–Tinsley road, via Whiston cross-roads to the Great North Road at Bawtry (now the A631), and four years later the road from Tinsley to Rotherham and Doncaster (now the A630) was turnpiked. At the same time, the Attercliffe-Worksop road (now the A57) was improved by another turnpike trust. These turnpike roads and the Don Navigation were the principal transport arteries until the coming of the railways at the beginning of Queen Victoria's reign.

The turnpike road across Attercliffe Common was the scene of the valley's best remembered incident from the past. In February 1791 Spence Broughton and John Oxley stole the Rotherham mail. They, and Thomas Shaw, were arrested in London some months later after another mail robbery. Oxley escaped from prison, but Shaw and Broughton were taken to York Assizes to be tried. Shaw saved his own neck by informing on Broughton, who was publicly hanged outside York prison (now the Castle Museum) on 14 April 1792. His body was then brought to the scene of his crime on Attercliffe Common, where it was hung in chains as a grisly warning to others. Enormous crowds turned up to see the spectacle. Broughton's bones and the remnants of his clothes were still on view in 1817 and the gibbet was not dismantled until ten years later. The memory of the event is perpetuated by the name Broughton Lane.

The improved transport facilities of the middle years of the eighteenth century signalled the beginnings of great industrial changes. The most momentous was Benjamin Huntsman's invention of a high quality cast steel, which he poured from heated clay crucibles into moulds. Huntsman was born in Epworth in 1704 of Quaker parents. He became a clock maker in Doncaster, but found that the 'blister steel' which was made in cementation furnaces was of insufficient quality for his springs and pendulums. He therefore began to experiment, remelting the cut-off ends of bars of blister steel in small pots, or crucibles, similar to those used by gold-smiths and glassmakers. A deep bed of coke served as his fuel. Huntsman's chief problem was in making crucibles which would stand the hot fire that was necessary for the melting of steel. Similar pots made from Bolsterstone clay were used during the 1740s at the nearby Catcliffe glass furnace (which still stands alongside the Parkway as it nears the M1), but it is known that Huntsman imported at least some of his crucibles from Holland. A melt lasted three to four hours, sometimes longer, after which the pots were lifted manually from the holes by giant pairs of tongs and the steel poured into moulds.

Figure 12. Treading the clay for making crucibles. This twentieth-century photograph shows how the original method of treading clay into a texture suitable for the making of crucibles was still used almost two centuries after Benjamin Huntsman's invention of crucible steel.

As we have seen, the first cementation furnace in south Yorkshire had been at work in 1642. By the 1730s the town of Sheffield had two small steel works and others had been built in the countryside to the south-east of the town. John Fell had added steel making to the activities of the partnership based at Attercliffe Forge. The total output of these works was modest; the Sheffield–Rotherham region was not a major centre of steel production before Huntsman's discovery. The success of his experiments began the transformation of the area into the major steel-producing centre of the world. For over a hundred years, until Bessemer's converter revolutionized production, the crucible method was the only way of making an ingot of steel.

Huntsman moved from Doncaster to Handsworth in 1742. He struggled to perfect his method in premises that were demolished about 1933 and which are known only from an old photograph and a watercolour painting. In 1751, finding that his experiments were successful and his business expanding, he moved to a larger building on the east side of Attercliffe Green. He abandoned clockmaking and became a full-time steel maker. One of his best customers was the famous Birmingham firm of Boulton & Watt, manufacturers of rotary steam engines. The firm of B. Huntsman, Limited, which was run by his descendants, always headed its stationery, 'Established 1751'. The move to Attercliffe was in the same year as the opening of the Don Navigation just down the road at Tinsley.

Huntsman stayed at Attercliffe Green for at least twelve, but no more than nineteen years, for by 1770 he had moved a short distance to premises on the other side of the road, a little further in the Darnall direction. These premises were known later as Huntsman's Row and were occupied by the firm until 1899, when a new works was opened in Coleridge Road, nearer Sheffield. On the gable end of a building next to Huntsman's Row, now the Britannia Inn, is the date '1772', allegedly made of steel by Benjamin Huntsman himself, and supposed to his residence in his last years.

Figure 13. Benjamin Huntsman's house. The Britannia Inn on Worksop Road, Attercliffe, was formerly the house built by Benjamin Huntsman in 1772, after he had moved a short distance from his original property nearby. The gable end on the right is inscribed '1772' in large letters, reputedly made from Huntsman's own steel.

In time, the invention of crucible steel came to be seen as the major cause of Sheffield and Rotherham's pre-eminence as a steel manufacturing district, but Huntsman was content to run a relatively small business that brought him modest prosperity. A memorial in the churchyard at Hill Top reads: 'Benjamin Huntsman of Attercliffe, steel refiner. Died June 20, 1776, aged 72 years'. Upon his death, he was succeeded by his son, William Huntsman (1733–1809), whom he had apprenticed to a button maker. The first Sheffield trade and commercial directory, of 1774, records the firm of Huntsman & Asline, button makers, in Jehu Lane, central Sheffield. Buttons made of crucible steel did not blister, so the business prospered. However, buttons formed only a part of the market for Huntsman's 'cast steel'. The real value of the invention lay in the production of tools, dies, and, above all, rolls. In the next Sheffield directory—that of 1787—Huntsman & Asline were listed as steel refiners. They rivalled Richard Swallow at Attercliffe Forge and Booth & Co. at Brightside Forge as the major firms in the eastern part of the parish of Sheffield before the massive development of the valley by Cammell, Vickers, Jessop, Firth and Brown, once the railway from Rotherham to Sheffield had been opened through Brightside in 1837.

Figure 14. Huntsman's works at Attercliffe in 1787. The characteristic chimneys of cementation furnaces appear on the left, those of the crucible furnaces on the right.

The stewards of the Earls of Shrewsbury had continued to run Attercliffe Forge and their other ironworks until the death of Earl Gilbert, the last lord to live in Sheffield. From 1618 onwards the Copleys, a gentry family of Sprotborough and Wadworth, near Doncaster, gradually acquired a monopoly of iron production in south Yorkshire. After the death of Lionel Copley in 1675, a syndicate of gentry ironmasters, led by the Spencers of Cannon Hall, Cawthorne, ran the business until the middle years of the eighteenth century. Attercliffe Forge became the responsibility of John Fell (1666–1724), who had previously been at Wortley Forge. He was known as the clerk, but was effectively the manager and a shareholder. His younger brother Thomas worked for him for a while, but in 1699 was in Jamaica selling Attercliffe goods. Iron forged at Attercliffe during the last decade of the seventeenth century was exported via Bawtry to the east coast ports and London

Figure 15. Portrait of William Huntsman.

and carried over land to many of the market towns of northern England. Production rose to 200 tons a year, but by the 1720s much of this trade had been lost to coke-made pig iron. The Upper Hammer was converted into a cutlers' grinding wheel about 1715, then in 1746 into a slitting mill to make nails, like the earlier mills at Wortley, Masbrough and Renishaw.

John Fell was probably a Quaker, and was possibly connected to the Quaker Fells of Westmorland. He married Ellen, the sister of Gamaliel Milner, the Quaker gentleman and ironmaster of Burton Grange, near Barnsley, but upon his death he was buried not in a Quaker burial ground but in Sheffield parish churchyard. His son, John Fell II (1696–1762), who became a Church Burgess (the body responsible for the maintenance of Sheffield Parish Church and for other charitable purposes), built 'a handsome brick house with spacious gardens' known as New Hall, Attercliffe, which must have seemed far more elegant than what had by then become old-fashioned halls at Carbrook and Attercliffe. New Hall has been demolished, but is commemorated by the name of a road. Although John Fell II married twice, he had no children, so he was succeeded at both the hall and the forge by his adopted son, Richard Swallow, who successfully adapted Attercliffe Forge to the new techniques of coke smelting and ensured its survival into the nineteenth century as one of south Yorkshire's major ironworks.

East of the Wicker, the river Don provided water-power for several other industrial sites. First came the Walk Mill, a fulling mill to which weavers brought their cloth. The 'Walkemullekerre' (the marshy ground around the Walk Mill) was recorded in 1442, but in the seventeenth century the mill was converted into two cutlers' grinding wheels. The site has been built over, but the weir is still visible from Effingham Street. Next came the works that was referred to in 1578 as Attercliffe Corn Mill, but which was known later as Royds Mill, probably because John Rodes became tenant of both the corn mill and an adjacent cutlers' wheel in the early seventeenth century. From the beginning of the eighteenth century until 1761 the site was leased by William Burton, father and son, members of a north Derbyshire lead-smelting family; the name Burton Weir is still in use. Later, it became a large ironworks belonging to Booth, Binks and Hartop, a leading firm of local ironmasters.

The Don then proceeded through Salmon Pastures to the Upper and Nether Hammers. Salmon Pastures has passed into Sheffield mythology as the heavily industrialized site that once was so idyllically rural that salmon could be seen leaping up the river. It is true that in 1637 John Harrison's survey mentions salmon amongst the fish in the local rivers, but the place-name was not recorded before 1760 and it is just as likely that these river-side pastures took their name from the Salmon family who were Sheffield residents in the seventeenth and eighteenth centuries. The river continued on its way to power the Brightside corn mill, where an adjoining cutlers' grinding wheel was recorded from the sixteenth century onwards. The corn mill became a forge, which was known as Brightside Tilt in 1738, before it was expanded into a major ironworks by Booth & Co. in the late 1750s. Further downstream was the Parker Wheel, which was a cutlers' grinding wheel in the seventeenth century, but which was converted into the Brightside Paper Mill in 1750. These were the various works whose source of water power the Duke of Norfolk had been so concerned to protect when he stopped the Don Navigation at Tinsley.

Much of Sheffield's early industrial development was based on water power. Steam power was first used locally to work the pumps that drained the deeper coal mines. Thomas Jeffreys's map of Yorkshire (1771) marks a 'Fire Engine' on Attercliffe or Darnall Common, probably the Newcomen-type engine that drained the Greenland Colliery. Another steam engine was installed in 1790 at the Duke of Norfolk's Attercliffe Colliery, a little further north. Ten years later, this colliery was producing over 44,000 tons of coal per annum. The Duke of Norfolk's pits operated on a large scale and were amongst the most up-to-date in the country in the last quarter of the eighteenth century, when the famous engineer, John Curr, from County Durham, was in charge. Coal was

Figure 16. Cementation furnaces. These two furnaces formed part of Huntsman's works at Attercliffe. The rhubarb suggests why the site became known as Huntsman's Gardens.

raised from the mines in Sheffield Park and on Attercliffe Common by 'drawing machines' and taken down to the Don Navigation on iron rails. The scale of the enterprise in the late eighteenth century was such that shafts at Park Colliery were up to 120 yards deep, and at Attercliffe Colliery between 80 and 100 yards. A drainage sough over 1500 yards long crossed Attercliffe Common from Darnall Colliery to the river Don. The extension of the Don navigation from Tinsley wharf to the Canal Basin in Sheffield in 1819 enabled the Norfolk estate to sell its coal at competitive prices much further afield.

Figure 17. Sheffield Canal Basin. This engraving from *The Mirror* periodical in 1826 shows the Terminal Warehouse as the centrepiece of the Canal Basin a few years after its opening.

The increasing pace of industrialization in the late eighteenth century was also evident from the scale of operations of the iron manufacturers and coal owners, John Booth of the Brushes, William Binks of Darnall, and John Hartop of Brightside. In 1784 Booth, Binks and Hartop installed a steam engine to pump water out of their mines. Four years later, they purchased a Boulton & Watt engine. John Booth was a partner of Samuel and Aaron Walker at their Masbrough ironworks and at Beeley Wood tilt and forge, as well as a partner with Binks and Hartop in the Park ironworks and coal mines, the Brightside Forge and Rolling Mill, the Nether Forge, and the Royds Mill and Wheel. Steam was also used to power William Hartop's Attercliffe Corn Mill, which was marked on the 1795 map of Sheffield parish between Oaks Green and Washford Bridge. It was rebuilt after a disastrous fire in 1804.

The pace of change quickened in the first half of the nineteenth century. A dramatic development in 1823 at the western end of the Lower Don Valley was the opening of Messrs Greaves's Sheaf Works, built at a cost of £50,000 as the first self-contained steel and tool works in Sheffield. It converted and melted its own steel and made its own tools, as well as manufacturing razors, penknives and other cutlery wares, particularly for the American market. The works opened four years after the opening of

Figure 18. Messrs Greaves's Sheaf Works. This view, taken shortly after the railway was opened in 1849, gives a strong impression of the size of the largest works in Sheffield before steel works were built further down the valley.

the Sheffield Canal, which had finally linked the town with the Don Navigation at Tinsley. The main office block in Maltravers Street, which is all that is left of the buildings by the canal basin, has now been renovated as part of the Victoria Quays development. The Sheaf Works once had the largest collection of cementation furnaces in Sheffield and was on a much bigger scale than any business seen in Sheffield before.

In the half century or so before the foundation of the great steel works in the east end of Sheffield parish, increasing opportunities for employment enabled the population to grow quickly. In 1801 the population of Attercliffe-cum-Darnall township was 2281; twenty years later it had reached 3172; and by 1841 it was 4156. It was to expand at an even faster rate as the district was changed out of all recognition in the second half of the century.

As the Lower Don Valley became more industrialized and populous, its character changed in other ways too. Large grants from the government's 'Million Act' (1818) had funded the building of Christ Church, Attercliffe (by 1826), together with St George's, St Phillip's and St Mary's in Sheffield. The old chapel of St Lawrence at Tinsley was enlarged in 1838 and rebuilt in 1877–79, and new churches were also built at Darnall and Brightside. Despite this activity, the majority of people in the huge parish of Sheffield did not attend church or chapel. In 1851, for instance, Christ Church, Attercliffe had a congregation of 138 in the morning and 116 in the evening, with 229 children at Sunday School. These attendances were high by modern standards, but they represented a small proportion of the local population.

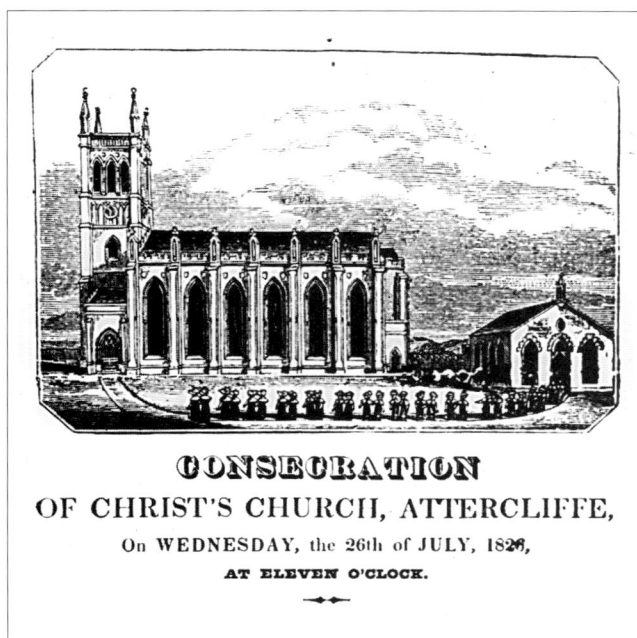

CONSECRATION OF CHRIST'S CHURCH, ATTERCLIFFE, On WEDNESDAY, the 26th of JULY, 1826, AT ELEVEN O'CLOCK.

Figure 19. Christ Church, Attercliffe. An advertisement for the consecration of the new church in 1826.

The Sheffield Register for 1 February 1792 noted, however, that:

> By the annual Report of the Sunday Schools at the village of Attercliffe...it appears that 120 poor boys and girls, upon an average, receive instruction from their benevolent institution. It was commenced in 1785 and has greatly improved the morals of the children, as may be seen by their constantly decent and orderly behaviour.

The Nonconformists also had their Sunday Schools. By the middle of the nineteenth century, chapel goers in Attercliffe could choose from the Zion Chapel (Independent or Congregationalist; founded in 1793, rebuilt in 1805 and again in 1863), the Salem Chapel (another Independent or Congregationalist group founded in 1828), the Wesleyan Methodists (established in 1835), or the Methodist New Connexion (founded in 1836). The Wesleyan Methodists also had chapels at Darnall and Grimesthorpe, and the Independents had a congregation at Brightside.

As the population of the Lower Don Valley expanded, these public buildings served as social centres as well as places of worship. The new brick houses, shops and pubs that added to the sense of change filled the spaces in and around the old settlements. The rows of terraced houses that characterized the district in later times were not yet built. A view of Sheffield in 1819, taken from Attercliffe Road, shows that countryside still separated the town from the villages and hamlets in the eastern part of the parish. The greatest changes were yet to come.

Though continuity rather than change is the major theme of the early history of the Lower Don Valley, we have seen that long before the railway from Sheffield to Rotherham was constructed in 1837, the district had undergone considerable alterations. We have noted the importance of the ironworks which had been erected in the valley as early as the 1570s, the revolution begun by Benjamin Huntsman, who had made crucible steel at Attercliffe Green from 1751, the improved transport facilities of the River Don Navigation and the turnpike roads, which had encouraged further commercial development, and the ways that old industrial sites along the river had been enlarged and put to new uses in the late-eighteenth and

Figure 20. View of Sheffield from Attercliffe Road, 1819. Edward Blore's view was taken in the year when the canal finally reached Sheffield. The rural nature of the journey from Attercliffe past Salmon Pastures is sharply contrasted with the smoke of Sheffield industries.

early-nineteenth centuries. Meanwhile, the cutlers and scissorsmiths pursued their ancient trades, in much greater numbers than before. By the middle of the nineteenth century the Lower Don Valley had long had an industrial tinge to its rural character. But these activities were modest in scale when compared with the enormous size of the enterprises that were soon to transform the district into one of the major manufacturing centres of the world.

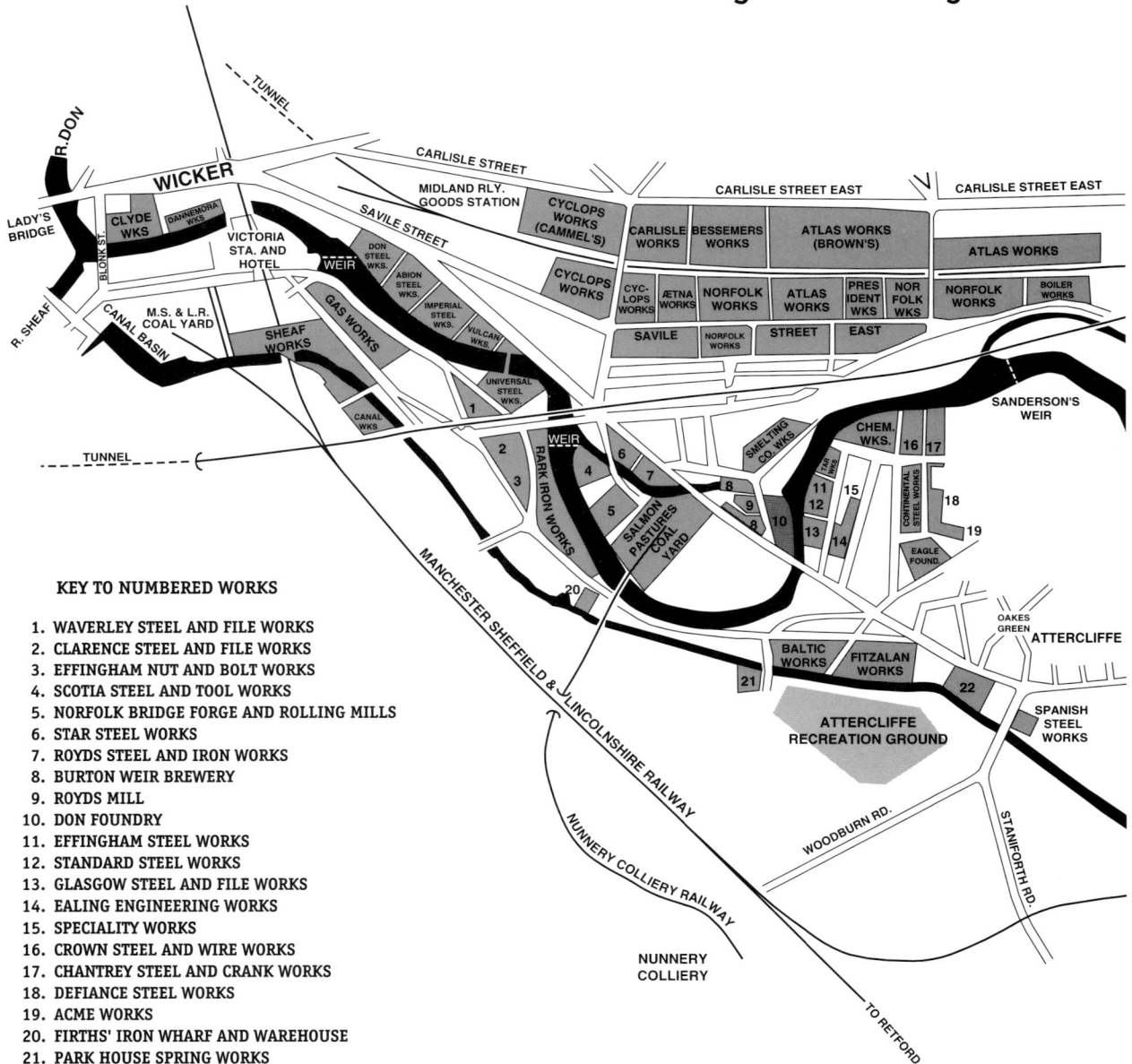

R. DON

R. SHEAF

LADY'S BRIDGE

TUNNEL

WICKER

BLONK ST.

CLYDE WKS

DANNEMORA WKS.

VICTORIA STA. AND HOTEL

M.S. & L.R. COAL YARD

CANAL BASIN

SHEAF WORKS

CARLISLE STREET

MIDLAND RLY. GOODS STATION

SAVILE STREET

WEIR

DON STEEL WKS.

ABION STEEL WKS.

IMPERIAL STEEL WKS.

VULCAN WKS.

GAS WORKS

CANAL WKS.

UNIVERSAL STEEL WKS.

CYCLOPS WORKS (CAMMEL'S)

CYCLOPS WORKS

CARLISLE STREET EAST

CARLISLE STREET EAST

CARLISLE WORKS

BESSEMERS WORKS

ATLAS WORKS (BROWN'S)

ATLAS WORKS

CYC-LOPS WKS.

ÆTNA WKS.

NORFOLK WORKS

ATLAS WORKS

PRES-IDENT WKS

NOR FOLK WKS

NORFOLK WORKS

BOILER WORKS

SAVILE

NORFOLK WORKS

STREET

EAST

SANDERSON'S WEIR

TUNNEL

WEIR

PARK IRON WORKS

SALMON PASTURES COAL YARD

SMELTING CO. WKS

CHEM. WKS.

TAR WKS

CONTINENTAL STEEL WORKS

EAGLE FOUND.

1
2
3
4
5
6
7
8
8
9
10
11
12
13
14
15
16
17
18
19
20

OAKES GREEN

ATTERCLIFFE

MANCHESTER SHEFFIELD & LINCOLNSHIRE RAILWAY

NUNNERY COLLIERY RAILWAY

NUNNERY COLLIERY

TO RETFORD

BALTIC WORKS

FITZALAN WORKS

21

22

SPANISH STEEL WORKS

ATTERCLIFFE RECREATION GROUND

WOODBURN RD.

STANIFORTH RD.

KEY TO NUMBERED WORKS

1. WAVERLEY STEEL AND FILE WORKS
2. CLARENCE STEEL AND FILE WORKS
3. EFFINGHAM NUT AND BOLT WORKS
4. SCOTIA STEEL AND TOOL WORKS
5. NORFOLK BRIDGE FORGE AND ROLLING MILLS
6. STAR STEEL WORKS
7. ROYDS STEEL AND IRON WORKS
8. BURTON WEIR BREWERY
9. ROYDS MILL
10. DON FOUNDRY
11. EFFINGHAM STEEL WORKS
12. STANDARD STEEL WORKS
13. GLASGOW STEEL AND FILE WORKS
14. EALING ENGINEERING WORKS
15. SPECIALITY WORKS
16. CROWN STEEL AND WIRE WORKS
17. CHANTREY STEEL AND CRANK WORKS
18. DEFIANCE STEEL WORKS
19. ACME WORKS
20. FIRTHS' IRON WHARF AND WAREHOUSE
21. PARK HOUSE SPRING WORKS
22. ATTERCLIFFE STEEL WORKS

East End of Sheffield, c. 1885

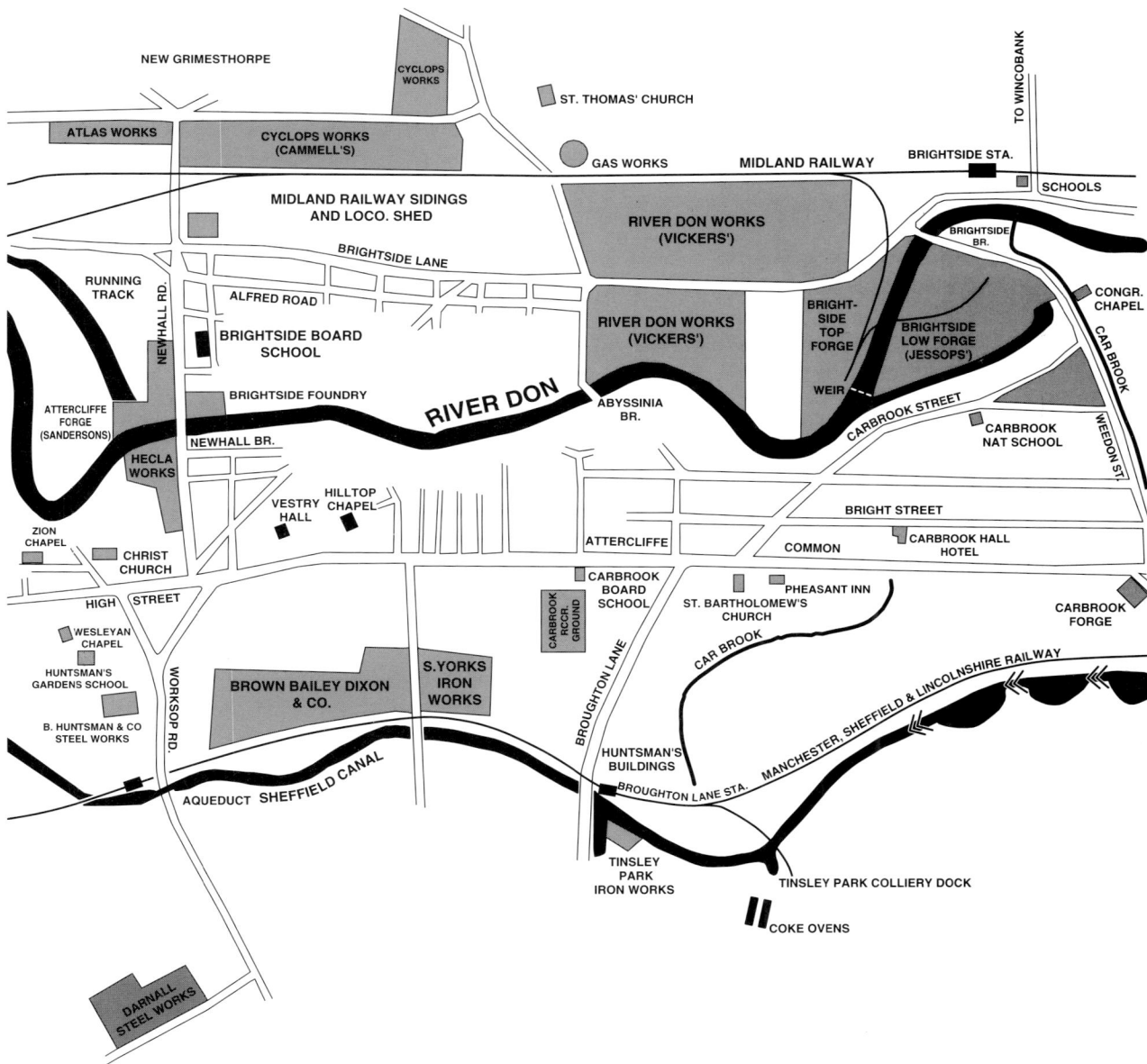

NEW GRIMESTHORPE

CYCLOPS WORKS

ATLAS WORKS

CYCLOPS WORKS (CAMMELL'S)

St. Thomas' Church

GAS WORKS

MIDLAND RAILWAY

BRIGHTSIDE STA.

SCHOOLS

MIDLAND RAILWAY SIDINGS AND LOCO. SHED

RIVER DON WORKS (VICKERS')

BRIGHTSIDE BR.

CONGR. CHAPEL

BRIGHTSIDE LANE

RUNNING TRACK

NEWHALL RD.

ALFRED ROAD

BRIGHTSIDE BOARD SCHOOL

RIVER DON WORKS (VICKERS')

BRIGHT-SIDE TOP FORGE

BRIGHTSIDE LOW FORGE (JESSOPS')

CAR BROOK

BRIGHTSIDE FOUNDRY

RIVER DON

ABYSSINIA BR.

WEIR

CARBROOK STREET

WEEDON ST.

ATTERCLIFFE FORGE (SANDERSONS)

NEWHALL BR.

HECLA WORKS

VESTRY HALL

HILLTOP CHAPEL

CARBROOK NAT SCHOOL

ZION CHAPEL

CHRIST CHURCH

ATTERCLIFFE

BRIGHT STREET

COMMON

CARBROOK HALL HOTEL

HIGH   STREET

WORKSOP RD.

CARBROOK BOARD SCHOOL

CARBROOK RCCR. GROUND

St. Bartholomew's Church

PHEASANT INN

CARBROOK FORGE

WESLEYAN CHAPEL

HUNTSMAN'S GARDENS SCHOOL

BROWN BAILEY DIXON & CO.

S.YORKS IRON WORKS

BROUGHTON LANE

CAR BROOK

B. HUNTSMAN & CO STEEL WORKS

AQUEDUCT SHEFFIELD CANAL

HUNTSMAN'S BUILDINGS

BROUGHTON LANE STA.

MANCHESTER, SHEFFIELD & LINCOLNSHIRE RAILWAY

TINSLEY PARK IRON WORKS

TINSLEY PARK COLLIERY DOCK

COKE OVENS

DARNALL STEEL WORKS

TO WINCOBANK

Sheffield's East End

Martin Olive

In 1837, as work progressed on the Sheffield and Rotherham Railway, a start seems to have been made on Savile Street East, parallel with the railway about 250 yards to the south east. Spear and Jackson, the famous saw makers, immediately moved out from the town and founded their Aetna Works in the middle of the fields and at the far end of the road. They were to remain in isolation for the best part of a decade. The opening of the railway in 1838 had little other immediate effect on the industrial life of the valley. Sheffield had been left at the country end of a branch line from the main route to the North, and it looked at first as if it would be Rotherham

Figure 21. Charles Cammell's Cyclops Works seen in 1845 from Carlisle Street. The picture demonstrates the importance of the link with the Sheffield and Rotherham Railway. The felling of the tree and gathering in of the last hay crop symbolize the rapid transition of the site from rural idyll to hive of heavy industry.

that would reap the advantage of improved communications. The most vital imports for the steel industry were Swedish iron bars which arrived by canal and continued to do so until long into the railway age.

Nevertheless the sudden worldwide expansion of railways created a demand for exactly the sort of crucible steel which Sheffield knew how to produce better than anyone else. Steel was wanted for springs, wheels and other locomotive parts, and the machine tools to make them. Firms in the town centre were quick to exploit the demand; John Brown of Rockingham Street invented the conical spring buffer which he was soon dispatching (often by road) to far flung systems. After he had been knighted in 1868, he incorporated the buffer, as a token of gratitude, into his coat of arms. It was to meet the demands of this railway trade that steel firms needed to expand quickly. Land in the town centre was getting scarce and expensive; along Savile Street there was open space and landowners were tractable. It was level and next to the railway, which could bring in coke and coal and carry away the finished products. By 1840 the Rotherham line was linked to Euston, Leeds and Birmingham. In 1845 the Woodhead Tunnel was completed, opening up a direct route to Manchester, Liverpool and the Americas, and two years later this route was linked to Savile Street by a short, steep and lethal incline under Spital Hill. By 1863 Savile Street had pushed through to join up with Brightside Lane and steel works extended in an almost unbroken line as far as Brightside Bridge. At the Sheffield end, the works now straddled the railway and formed an equally solid line along Carlisle Street.

In 1846 Charles Cammell established his Cyclops Works on the Sheffield side of Spear and Jackson. This is commonly reckoned the first of the great steel firms. The size was unprecedented in Sheffield but even so Cammell seems not to have anticipated the extent of his success. His works had soon crossed the railway; for further extension it was necessary to leapfrog over Mark Firth and John Brown and set up further down the line at Grimesthorpe. Cammell was an outsider who had come from Hull as a young man and did well selling files for Ibbotson Bros. When Ibbotsons fell into financial trouble, he teamed up with their cashier and started a steel and file business. At Cyclops Works railway parts, rails and later armaments were to make him one of the richest men in Sheffield. During this time he was closely associated with George Wilson, a Scotsman who married into the family and became managing director of the firm and remained in charge after Cammell's death in 1879. Cammell put some of his wealth to acquiring country estates and lived for a time as squire of Norton Hall. By 1864 Cammell's was employing nearly 4000 men and making an annual profit of about £50,000. Little of this found its way to local charities, and Cammell took no conspicuous part in public life outside Norton, where he planned to rest in a mausoleum. It was never completed, and he was in fact buried at Hathersage.

The next major arrivals in Savile Street were by contrast a strong family team who endeared themselves above all to their contemporaries for their public spirit and ready response to good causes. Thomas Firth was born in Pontefract but came to Sheffield and became head melter for Sandersons in West Street, a well-paid position which enabled him to give his two eldest sons a reasonable education to the age of 14, after which they joined him at the steel works. Mark, the salesman, and Thomas, the practical melter, soon left to found their own firm and persuaded their father to join them. In 1855, after the father's death, all five brothers established the Norfolk Works on Savile Street. A cousin was installed in a cottage at the works to act as caretaker and pay the wages. Unlike Cammell, Mark Firth cultivated a family atmosphere in the works, paying especial respect to the skilled melters who had followed him from Sandersons, men like Josie Richardson, the 21 stone giant who presided over the commissioning feast at the Norfolk Works. To the end Firth liked to take his midday meal at the works, but seems to have been almost equally at home in Court circles where he especially cultivated Prince Leopold. He entertained the Prince of Wales in 1875 at his residence, Oakbrook at Ranmoor, when he was Mayor of Sheffield, while Prince Leopold and John Ruskin, among others, were his guests at the opening of Firth College in 1879. The College reflected his interest in technical education; other endowments included chapels and almshouses. The Firths had a shrewd eye for a bargain; part of their commercial success in the 1850s stemmed from their cornering the tight market in Swedish iron bars. Their extensive local property speculations included the Page Hall Estate within a mile of the works. Half of this Mark Firth laid out as a public park for the East End, and had it opened in 1875 by the Prince of Wales. Publicity was another Firth instinct. Mark died in 1880, after suffering a stroke at the works. He was succeeded by his brother Charles Edward and later by his son. Considering their very high profile, Firth's remained relatively small and highly specialized.

In 1856 John Brown moved out from Rockingham Street. He had the advantage of buying a virtually brand new works from a bankrupt concern at a knock down price. John Brown introduced puddling, a process used for producing wrought iron, and which with modifications could be applied to steel. The steel was of a lower grade than crucible steel, but much more affordable, and opened up new markets such as rails. The furnaces were also suitable for producing wrought iron armour plates for warships, a product which Brown pioneered in this country and which was to bring enormous wealth to the East End by 1914. The downside was that puddling was a thoroughly nasty process, demanding great physical strength of the puddler who had to endure extreme heat and noxious fumes. John Brown's furnaces produced a particular black and pungent smoke which gave Carlisle Street the reputation of being separated from Hell by a tissue paper and drove the middle classes off the neighbouring slopes. To make his plate Brown invested in huge steam hammers and the type of rolling mill that was to become a speciality of Davy Bros at Foley Street. By 1867 John Brown's employed some 3300 men and his turnover was nearly £1 million.

John Brown took an active interest in his workforce, to the extent of establishing a school for lads working at the works and encouraging prayer meetings during the lunch hours. His most conspicuous memorial in the East End was the huge All Saints' Church whose spire long dominated the skyline above the works and whose Sunday schools once enrolled pupils in thousands. Like Mark Firth he was active on the Town Council and became Mayor in 1863. He was also the first chairman of the Sheffield School Board. He raised two companies of volunteer Hallamshire Rifles from the Atlas Works, for which patriotic gesture he was commissioned to the rank of Captain. He was knighted in 1868. For all his achievements his later life was rather a sad one. Royalty never visited his palatial residence in Endcliffe. Profits at the Atlas Works were slow to respond to heavy investment and in 1868 he made an acrimonious departure from his own firm. His nephew and heir died young, though the firm Sir John started for him in Attercliffe eventually prospered as Brown Bayley's. John Brown died in Kent in relative poverty in 1896.

A highly significant arrival on Carlisle Street next to John Brown in 1858 was Henry Bessemer. His converters were capable of producing steel better and more quickly than by puddling, and at even less cost. It was not long before John Brown was round making enquiries. For twenty years Brown and Cammell used the Bessemer process to supply the world with steel rails and material for heavy engineering.

Savile Street had by now reached Brightside Lane with continuous heavy steel works extending from the Wicker Station to Grimesthorpe and across the railway to Carlisle Street and Carlisle Street East.

The Vickers were a long established local family whose background was corn milling. The previous generation adapted itself and converted its mill to the more profitable business of steel. Tom Vickers was a dedicated technical steelmaker who devoted the profits from very successful trading in America to the development of the latest German technology. A notable advance was achieved at the old River Don Works at Millsands with the casting of steel church bells. The fashion for this product proved short-lived, but more utilitarian and equally lucrative applications of the technology were soon found. By 1863 they had outgrown Millsands and moved out beyond John Brown's onto Brightside Lane where they set up a new River Don works between the railway and the river. Tom's brother Albert was a suave business dealer who was the brain behind the spectacular conversion of the Sheffield steel firm into a multi-national munitions supplier. In 1367 Vickers ranked in size below Cammell's and Brown's but above Firth's, with about 1000 employees.

Tom and Albert Vickers were almost a generation younger than the other steel pioneers of the East End and lived well into the golden age of the early twentieth century. Tom was Master Cutler in 1875 and Colonel of the Infantry Volunteers; Albert moved closer to the sources of finance in London.

Beyond the River Don's Heritage Canyon lies the river, Brightside Weir and Brightside Bridge. Here were the Brightside wheels, one a mediaeval corn mill and the other a cutler's wheel from the seventeenth century. Both had been converted by Booth and Co. into a forge and tilt, still using water power. By 1840 the works were leased to a small firm of steel makers in Furnival Street belonging to William Jessop. The firm advanced rapidly as crucible steel suppliers particularly through the salesmanship of William's sons Sidney and Thomas in America. For a short period in the early 1850s Jessop's, with 10 furnaces and 120 crucible holes, were the largest steel makers in the country. Thomas, who outlived his brothers, had lived as a boy in a cottage in the Brightside works. Apprenticed to a toolmaker, he was remembered as a genial and warmhearted soul. He was Mayor in 1864 and was the principal benefactor to the Jessop Hospital for Women. He retired to Endcliffe Grange where he died in 1887 but had bought extensive estates in the East Riding. His son William much preferred the country life to the chair of his father's firm.

All this progress had taken place on the Brightside half of the Valley. As late as 1868 Attercliffe could still be described as a village. Its steel works were of an earlier generation and on a smaller scale, like Huntsman's on Worksop Road. There were a few newcomers like Beardshaw's Baltic Works by the canal side, and most significantly Sanderson's crucible shop,

Figure 22. The Brightside Works in 1858, looking up the Don with Weedon Street in the left foreground and Brightside Lane on the right. This was a nineteenth-century development of two ancient waterpowered industrial sites. The Low Works on the left employed water power for tilting well into the twentieth century. Many crucible furnace chimneys testify to Jessop's commitment to the Huntsman process. Note also the manager's house, in which the great Thomas Jessop himself spent his youth.

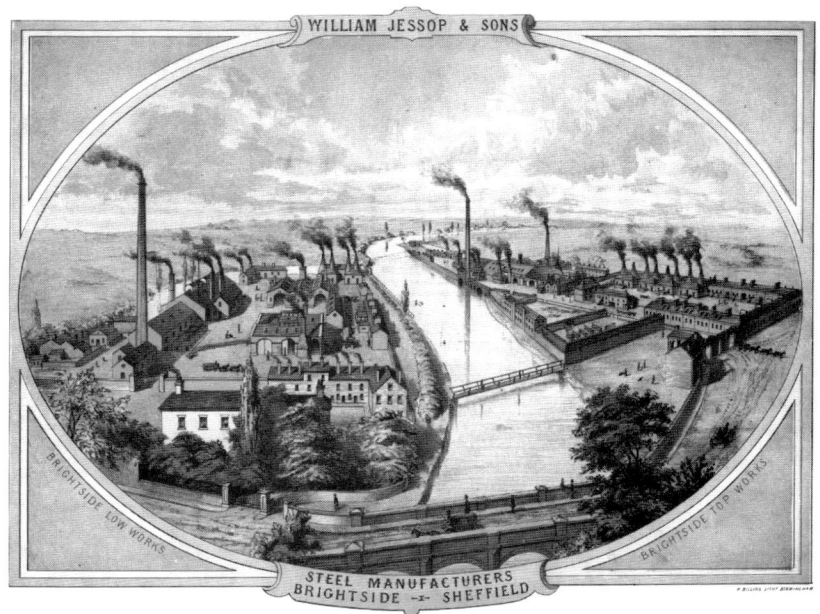

still standing on Darnall Road, which was second in size only to Jessop's. By comparison with the newcomers on Savile Street they were still small. What is also striking is that the families of the proprietors all chose to continue living in the village. There was still a range of handsome property for the wealthy, by all accounts. The Spencer's seventeenth-century hall still stood at the east end of the village, and the early eighteenth-century Carlton House towards the Sheffield end. The Misses Milner still occupied Milner House on Leeds Road. The Vicarage was 'snug as a finch's nest' in the trees adjoining the Church, and Mr V.G. Beardshaw of Baltic Works lived at Don Bank House hard by the windmill. At Woodburn Hall, towards the Park, lived that 'jolly old Pickwickian' William Brookes, basking in the celebrity accorded him from his brief appearance as 'Brookes of Sheffield' in 'Dombey and Son'. The most opulent local residence was New Hall, standing across the river in extensive grounds and reached from the village by a tree-lined avenue. John Sanderson, who died in 1852, was the last private resident. The house and estate were purchased by a firm called Hunt and Co. who seem originally to have had in mind a working man's alternative to the Botanical Gardens, with balloons, brass bands and, crucially, beer. There was also a cricket ground, a running track and a bowling green, and it was for sporting events, especially on the track, that New Hall was famed over the next 25 years, attracting crowds by excursion train from neighbouring towns. The respectable middle class disapproved of a venue associated with heavy betting and hard drinking. By 1880 the original New Hall had been replaced by a refreshment pavilion, but the gardens did not survive into the football age, being shortly afterwards bought by Robert Hadfield for an extension to his works though in the event the site was used for housing.

Figure 23. Workers at the Sheffield Smelting Company's works, Royds Lane. This industry prospered by collecting sweepings from the floors and benches of silversmiths' workshops and salvaging the precious metal content. It moved from Green Lane to Attercliffe in 1790. Latterly it was owned by the radical and nonconformist Wilson family who were enlightened and progressive employers. Many of these men were members of Hatfield House Primitive Methodist Church, Shiregreen.

After relatively slow growth during the previous decade, Attercliffe and Darnall doubled their population between 1861 and 1871 when the census recorded 26,969. For the next two decades it was to be the fastest grow- ing district in Sheffield. In 1861 there was a wide spread of occupations available. The centre of the village contained cutlers working in most tradi- tional branches of the trade as well as moulders, melters and forgers in iron and steel works. There was a very large number of blacksmiths, which term may have been used to cover the chain makers whose trade was an Attercliffe speciality. There was still some agriculture, though farmers worked on a small scale and sometimes had a second occupation; one was also registrar of births, marriages and deaths. In 1841 the Vicar, John Blackburn, described the occupations of the local juveniles. Boys found employment as milk boys, whose morals were very bad, and in the local earthenware potteries and brickyards. From the age of 6 or 7 they could be earning a few shillings picking shale in coke yards, potmaking, blowing bellows or striking for chain makers, while they were employed in the collieries as trappers, horse lads and 'ginnears', who tied and untied wagons to the haulage ropes. For girls there was less choice in the immediate vicin- ity. Too many, Blackburn complained, were having to travel to Sheffield to find work in hair seating, hardware, Britannia metal and silver plating, 'all sad demoralizing schools'.

Blackburn painted rather a jolly picture of the Attercliffe collier lads. They might be miserably underfed and forced to spend 13 hours a day underground, but he generally found them 'as happy to see to as kings', playing at quoits with horse shoes, at the fox geese board or catching colliery mice to take home for their cats. He was impressed with the way boys lucky enough to be provided with a piece of bread for dinner would share with those who had none. On the other hand they made little demand on his professional services, and wages of 3/- to 7/- a week were a powerful counterattraction in the eyes of their parents to his National School. Twenty years later all these trades were still found in the village, with the exception of the milk boys. By far the dominant occupation was coal mining. The pits at Tinsley Park and Carbrook, which in 1841 were leased by Booth & Co., were by 1861 worked by the Huntsman family. Francis Huntsman, last of the line to be brought up in Attercliffe, was a paternalistic employer, who paid for a school at Tinsley Park and sponsored the Attercliffe Working Men's Club.

Besides the National School next to the Church, Attercliffe had the old Town School, now relocated on Leeds Road. The Congregationals were the most expansionist denomination in the 1860s. Under the Rev. John Calvert a thriving and distinctively working-class religious community developed. Zion Chapel was rebuilt in 1863 in a style described as 'semi-Gothic', more often associated with public baths; it was large, with seats for 960. A school was also provided, where Sir Henry Coward, the famous choral conductor, started his teaching in 1872 under the easygoing Mr Bowker. Coward's possibly biased memories record a system under which Bowker took the fees and government grant, appointed pupil teachers as cheap labour and left them to sink or swim. Attercliffe had otherwise an ample range of amenities, with a post office and many retail shops, including drapers, several booksellers and a circulating library. A regular omnibus service to Sheffield was provided from 1855; briefly, passengers had a choice of first, second or third class. In 1864 the South Yorkshire Railway, now owners of the canal, used the adjacent land to construct a new line of railway from Meadowhall to Woodburn Junction, bringing South Yorkshire coal to their depot on the arches above the Canal Basin in Sheffield. The route was thriftily selected to avoid compulsory purchase of land and the consequent expense of an Act of Parliament. Though it passed through the village, Attercliffe was not at first provided with a station and intending passengers had to walk to Broughton Lane.

Only a few of the thousands of employees of the great works in Savile Street and Brightside Lane came from the Attercliffe side of the valley. Apart from several buildings along Carlisle Street (with beerhouses heavily represented) there is little evidence of residential development before the 1870s. Many families settled or remained in the Wicker district which was within walking distance of the great works for the men but was also convenient for the older industrial districts which offered a wider range of employment, especially for girls and women. If a family prospered, they would move a little further up the hill towards the superior terraces of Pitsmoor. Land Societies were active at Carbrook in the mid 1850s, when they bought up the Hall and its surrounding estate, and later developed New Grimesthorpe, the area including Carlisle Road and Adsetts Street. The Societies should in theory have produced a landscape of artisans' cottages standing in well-tended allotments, but except for a small estate at Carwood building activity was sluggish and when the houses arrived they were the drably uniform brick terraces favoured by speculative builders everywhere. New Grimesthorpe's first occupants were largely Black Country people, a community which in the 1870s found themselves much despised by their neighbours in old Grimesthorpe, who found their dialect unintelligible (it was thought to be a kind of German) and their manners uncouth.

Nor was there any conspicuous attempt by any of the steel magnates to create communities based on their works. Two firms made limited efforts to provide housing for their workers. Benjamin Huntsman & Co. built some rather spacious back-to-backs with generous gardens on Broughton Lane for miners at Tinsley Park, and much later Robert Hadfield built a row of rather drab 'model' dwellings, distinguished by large double porches, on Don Road, near his old Hecla works. John Brown's monumental church and schools could have become the focal point of a personal fiefdom, but it lacked a resident lord. Whereas the previous generation of steel magnates would have resided within sight of the works, the new breed set up house at Endcliffe, Ranmoor or Abbeydale in the western suburbs. Only Tom Vickers at Bolsover Hill and Charles Kayser at the Brushes preferred the eastern side of the town, but this was for the sake of their work rather than their workforce as both were notorious workaholics and were like as not to spend the night bedding down in the office.

Where did the new workforce come from? A core of skilled workers, crucible melters in particular, came from Sheffield. Puddling was a new skill to Sheffield and puddlers were recruited from ironworking districts, particularly Staffordshire. Some men brought young sons with them, and in 1863 the Children's Employment Commission found examples of 11 year olds working 12 hour shifts night or day, sometimes both together if the expected relief failed to materialize. Charles Cammell told the Commissioner that it would be 'tantamount to stopping our works' if he were to be prevented from employing children on night shifts. At Firth's and Brown's, as one might expect, they were officially more cooperative, though the management had no exact idea of working practices, which they regarded as the internal affair of each individual team. Apprentices were usually bound to fathers or relations, and employers accepted no liability for seeing they were properly trained and not overworked and underpaid. The replies of the boys interviewed reveal that some had started work in the West Midlands, others locally as collier lads. Though some were patently suffering from long hours, strenuous work and an unhealthy atmosphere, the East End works were no worse in this respect than those in the town centre. Fetching beer from the pubs on Carlisle Street was one of the more pleasant duties; steel melters were said to consume up to 16 pints a day. Each man had his own mug which the boy carried hooked to a long pole. Lunch was normally cooked at home and brought by one of the younger children during the school dinner hour, usually in a basin wrapped in a towel. Harry Brearley as a lad proved that any child could pass unquestioned through any steelworks as long as it was carrying a similar bundle.

The new works also required a large force of labourers, and there was continuous employment for bricklayers, joiners and furnace builders. Many young single men were attracted from agricultural counties, particularly Nottinghamshire and Lincolnshire. They would put up initially as lodgers or in boarding houses and at times of bad trade would return to their villages.

Figure 24. Steel melting team at Brown Bayleys', 1911. The team was the essential unit of production in the nineteenth-century steel works. The gaffer, or 'cod', on the left, negotiated with the management and was paid
weekly for the steel produced. The men received their wages from him on Friday nights, usually in the pub.
Highest wages went to the head melter, centre on the front row. He would be a man at the height of his skill and
physical strength. In his forties he would probably retire to a far less physically arduous job on the back row.

The delay in providing homes for steel workers largely spared the East End
the typical Sheffield court surrounded by back-to-back houses. In 1865
the Town Council introduced housing byelaws which prohibited further
construction of back-to-backs, and the houses which spread over
Brightside, Carbrook and the slopes above Carlisle Street conformed to the
new standards, if only just. The typical house was put up by a small speculative builder in a two-storey brick terrace, opening direct onto the street
with a jennel leading to a paved or asphalted yard at the back. There was
no garden and no garret. They filled in spaces between the works so tightly
that a terrace would often end abruptly against a towering gable wall of
corrugated iron.

By 1890 the character of the Lower Don Valley was firmly established.
The pattern of works, streets, schools, churches, chapels and pubs was to
last without major change until the 1960s. The great works dominated the

north side of the valley where land had been cheap and level and there was easy access to the Midland Railway. The works were the creation of individuals who had seen expansion as the way to acquiring great personal wealth. For the most part men of local families and comparatively humble origins, they were happy to trade with the world but their ambitions politically and socially were concentrated on Sheffield. Attercliffe, on the south side of the valley, was an ancient settlement and offered less scope for green field development, though it had the advantage of water and rail links. With the exception of Brown Bayley's, works here were on a smaller scale. Residential development continued to take place in Attercliffe up to 1914, while the old village centre developed facilities appropriate to a sizeable town. Carbrook was predominantly residential. There was still some open space between Carbrook and Tinsley Park where scruffy meadows merged into an untidy colliery landscape with small pits, spoil heaps and a few nests of miners' cottages among the remnants of the ancient woods. On the north side New Grimesthorpe had linked up with Burngreave, and was still a popular choice for newcomers to the East End. A community was also developing on the south side of Brightside Lane, including the old site of the Newhall Gardens.

Figure 25. Congestion at the Canal Wharf, 1889. The South Quay received iron bar and coal. Boats had to be moored five deep by the quayside and were unloaded laboriously by hand. A queue would be waiting below Tinsley Locks for space to be cleared at the Basin. By 1889 complaints by canal users had brought about the Sheffield and South Yorkshire Canal Act, which resulted in limited improvements, but never realized the new canal age of which its promoters had dreamed.

There was no plan whatsoever behind this. Town Council initiatives were confined to widening the Attercliffe Road and replacing Washford Bridge. They were also reluctantly drawn into the affairs of the Tramway Company. This concern had selected the routes to Brightside and Carbrook on a commercial basis and opened them in 1874. They proved no match for John Lambert's penny omnibus service on the Attercliffe Road, until the Council regulated the competition. In other respects the Council was less helpful. They set their faces against mechanical traction and insisted upon early morning cheap cars for workmen, but the two cars morning and evening which the company grudgingly provided cannot have had a major impact on working class travel habits.

It was occasionally possible for Council, Cutlers' Company and the leading manufacturers to combine in a common purpose. One such cause was the agitation for a ship canal in the 1880s. So far from the ports, Sheffield manufacturers found themselves at the mercy of the railway companies, who at that time managed the canal. A 300 ton boat would also solve the problem of conveying really large castings, which were over-size for the railways and had to be dragged across the Pennines by teams of traction engines. The scheme would have transformed the river northwards from Sanderson's weir into a huge inland port. In the event all that happened was that the Canal was partially liberated from railway control and some much needed additional warehousing was provided at the Canal Basin. A more successful venture was the Sheffield District Railway. This was a short line from Treeton to Brightside with a new station on Stevenson Road at Attercliffe. It was part of an ambitious scheme to break railway monopoly, but in this the steel barons of Sheffield were no match for the railway barons. It was useful as a link with the expanding Nottinghamshire coalfield and for a time carried a sparse suburban passenger service. In the meanwhile, not apparently connected with either proposal, the Duke of Norfolk had the Don diverted between Stevenson Road and Newhall Road. The old winding course under the cemetery was filled in with industrial waste and eventually occupied with extensions to

Hecla Works, while Attercliffe effectively lost its cliff.

The scale of steel making continued to grow, though not without interruption. The 1870s had seen the two largest companies, Brown's and Cammell's, supplying bulk steel to the world, thanks to their early investment in Bessemer converters. Siemens' open hearth process was likewise rapidly taken up by Vickers in 1871 and by Cammell's shortly afterwards. This had the advantage over Bessemer of being more controllable, but shared the disadvantage for Sheffield in requiring phosphor free pig iron. It was embraced with even more enthusiasm by Sheffield's competitors with ready supplies of ore and locations near to the sea. America was soon producing all the Bessemer and Siemens steel it needed and starting to export. The upshot was that Sheffield firms either had to transfer production or develop other specialities. Cammell's adopted both courses. Their entire Dronfield plant was moved in 1883 to Workington, close to the sea, and to the haematite mines and blast furnaces at Distington. Brown Bayley and Dixon failed to take either course, and went bankrupt in 1881. Brown's and Cammell's were already heavily into armour plate, while Firth's concentrated on gun barrels and projectiles. Vickers and Jessop's specialized in cast steel. Other firms, notably Samuel Osborn, concentrated on developments in tool steel. By 1890 Sheffield had virtually ceased to supply bulk steel to the world. Its ascendency was to be in high value special steels and was achieved through a combination of traditional skills and scientific research. For armour, projectiles and certain alloy steels Sheffield had become the world leader by 1914.

In 1875 Cammell's catalogue offered an armour plated fort complete with guns for immediate delivery; purchaser to prepare foundation. Armour plate evolved from wrought iron through composite iron and steel plates to all steel by 1890. Casting techniques developed to allow the production of tubes and gun barrels weighing up to a hundred tons or more and the technology was applied to sterns, rudders and propellers. Armaments was a business which involved continuous costly investment, Firth's repeatedly having to test their claim to make unstoppable shells

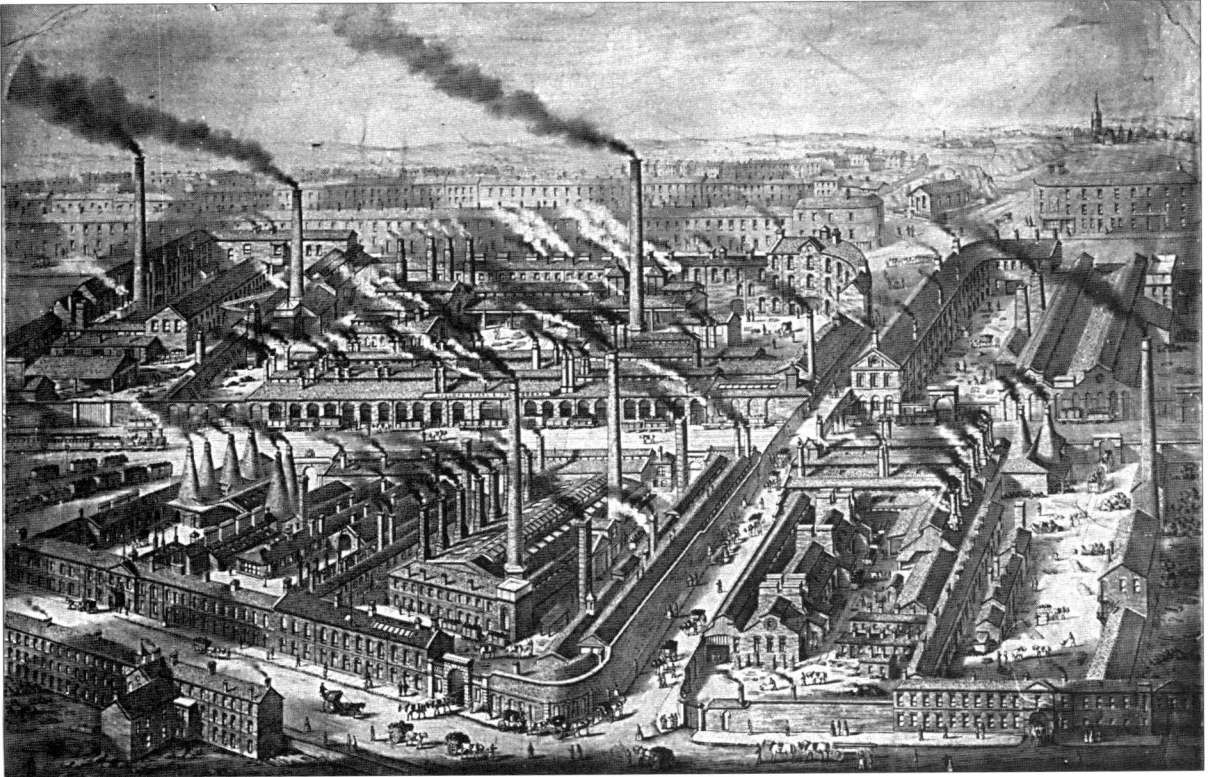

Figure 26. Cyclops Works, Charles Cammell and Co. c.1870, looking up Sutherland Street. Savile Street is on the bottom left and Savile Street East leads out of the picture on the right. Exports of railway materials were at their height and armaments were assuming a major role. Cyclops Works had expanded across Sutherland Street as far as Spear and Jackson and over the railway to Carlisle Street. Puddled and Bessemer steels were supplementing steel made by the traditional cementation and Huntsman processes. At the top of Sutherland Street the new All Saints' Church, paid for by John Brown, dominates the skyline. Charles Cammell gave rather more modest encouragement to Gower Street Wesley Reform Chapel at the foot of the hill.

against Brown's to produce impenetrable armour. This was quite a jolly game, usually carried out at Spithead with Krupp's joining in and the Admiralty acting as referee. But the Navy was an exacting customer and orders fluctuated with the demands of foreign policy. The biggest employers in the East End were heavily dependent on armaments. Geoffrey Tweedale shows that Cammell's directors were aware of the danger as early as the 1870s; some complained 'they were on a roundabout they dared not get off'. As it turned out the peace after the Boer War brought soup kitchens to Carbrook, a small foretaste of what was to happen after the Treaty of Versailles.

The great armament firms needed to protect their huge investments by securing their supplies of raw materials and acquiring engineering and shipbuilding firms to utilize the steels they produced. John Brown purchased Rotherham Main Colliery and Clydebank shipyards. Cammell's bought the Oaks Colliery at Barnsley and Lairds' shipyard at Birkenhead to add to their operations in Cumbria. Jointly the two Sheffield firms took over the Coventry Ordnance Company. Within Sheffield there were some mergers: Brown's with Firth's in 1902 and Jessop's with J.J. Saville in 1905.

The great empire builders of the period were Vickers under the rule of Colonel Tom and 'Don Alberto', a remarkable family team which stood out in an age when the professional manager was starting to dominate boardrooms. Tom solved the technical problems set by the military, while Albert conversed with governments and frequented the luxurious continental hotels where international arms dealers did their business. The firms which Vickers acquired in Britain included the Maxim Gun Company in Crayford, Kent, the Naval Construction and Armaments Company in Barrow and Wolseley Cars in Coventry. They were half owners of William Beardmore in Glasgow and Whitehead & Co., the torpedo makers of Weymouth and Fiume. Abroad they had interests in Spain, Italy, Japan, Russia and Turkey. By 1914 Vickers directly employed 22,000 people, of whom only 6000 worked in Sheffield, mostly at River Don Works. They were one of the largest companies in the UK, and the only one capable of designing, building and fitting out a battleship entirely on their own premises. Within Sheffield they were the largest employers, and shareholders could expect a return on average of 13.3 per cent. Albert Vickers found time to contest the Brightside parliamentary seat for the Conservatives, but was twice rebuffed. He did not realize his political ambitions till the end of the War, and then only by shifting to the safe Conservative seat of Ecclesall.

Vickers' shareholders had some reason for satisfaction, but there was one firm that put their profits in the shade. This was Hadfields Foundry which was started by Robert Hadfield, assistant overseer and rate collector for

Figure 27. Inside the West Forge at Cammell's Cyclops Works. Huge armour plates are being bent under the hydraulic press. The picture comes from a brochure which Cammell's issued about 1900 for circulation at home and abroad. The photographs were taken by Tulleys of Division Street, leading industrial photographers of their day.

Attercliffe, with John Mallaband, who had been a moulder for Vickers. They established the Hecla Works in 1872 on Newhall Road, and specialized in castings, developing the technique by the traditional means of trial and error. Robert Abbott Hadfield, Robert's son, was born in the Attercliffe Vestry Hall. As a teenager, he was fascinated by the scientific analysis of steel. He got his father to install a furnace in the basement of his home in Broomhill. The pursuit was both fashionable and timely. H.C. Sorby, born at Woodburn Hall and like Hadfield a native East Ender, had lectured to the Literary and Philosophical Society on his studies of the structure of steel as revealed through the microscope. Outside Sheffield,

Robert Mushet discovered how to make self-hardening steel by the addition of tungsten. His discovery was taken up about 1870 by Samuel Osborn of Clyde Works in the Wicker and rapidly spread to other Sheffield tool makers. This analytical approach led to the establishment of laboratories in the leading steel works, whose findings complemented the practical skills of the melter in detecting minute changes of colour or texture. It seems to have been pure thirst for knowledge, backed by his father's resources, that drove young Hadfield to discover the work hardening properties of manganese steel in 1882. Once he had made the discovery, he had to devote equal determination to finding a commercial application for it. It was ten years before it proved its worth for such applications as railway crossovers, excavator teeth and burglar-proof safes.

Investment in scientific research, so well exemplified by Hadfield, was vitally necessary to keep Sheffield steel technically ahead of foreign competition. The two main challenges from abroad were Krupp's invention of 'cemented plate' and the heat-treated high speed steel developed by Taylor and White at Bethlehem in the USA. Fortunately for Sheffield these potentially disastrous developments came in the 1890s when the flow of technical information was surprisingly unrestricted and Sheffield analysts were able to copy and soon to improve on both innovations.

Figure 28. Newhall Road, looking north, about 1900. Once a tree-lined private drive to the Fells' mansion, the road is now mainly distinguished by the original Hecla Works, named after a volcano in Iceland. Here Robert Hadfield and John Mallaband experimented with casting steel in 1872. Expansion to East Hecla took place in 1897.

Hadfields were probably the most innovative steel firm in the early 1900s. In 1897 they expanded onto a new site at East Hecla, just over the boundary into Tinsley. They developed other alloy steels, so that they could cast steel armour. They also developed projectiles. By 1914 no other shells could rival theirs in forcing their way through armour plate. Hadfield in many ways appears a slightly old-fashioned Victorian figure, equally successful as entrepreneur and practical inventor. He ran the firm as a one man show, and saw himself as an enlightened employer, a pioneer of the 48 hour week, encouraging sports and recreational activities and even dabbling in model housing. At all events, strike breakers never had to be recruited from distant parts and smuggled past the gates of East Hecla. The expansion paid off spectacularly. By 1914 Hadfields employed 5600 men, second only to Vickers, and was paying shareholders 25 per cent. Shares in Hadfields were unfortunately not easily come by; the majority belonged to R.A. Hadfield.

Figure 29. Inaugural electric tram at Carbrook, 9 September 1899. The Lord Mayor, Master Cutler and their relations are vying to be photographed at the controls. Electrification followed municipal purchase of the horse tramways and transformed their usefulness by reducing fares, vastly extending the system and providing services which catered for the working patterns of the East End.

Other steel makers who emerged to prominence at this period were Joseph Jonas, who founded the Continental Works at Attercliffe with Robert Colver in 1876, and W. Edgar Allen, who had evolved from a general agent into a specialist steel maker during the 1870s. Both men had strong continental connections and were highly innovative. Edgar Allen moved to Tinsley in 1891 and in 1910 built the first electric arc furnace in Sheffield. Jonas, born in Germany, was one of the few of the new breed of steel masters to follow the earlier tradition of service on the Town Council. He was Lord Mayor at the time of Edward VII's visit to Sheffield in 1905. Both were also supporters of technical education, contributing to the Technical College and later to the University.

Specialization, which required continuous investment in ever larger rolling mills and hydraulic presses, also prolonged the life of the crucible melting team which remained an economic way of producing small quantities of valuable special alloys. Even the largest firms often continued to offer a range of traditional Sheffield products, but not always using traditional skills. Firth's, for example, had a large file department at Norfolk Works, but by the 1890s it was largely mechanized and employed women on a semi-skilled basis. There were many jobs in the great works for unskilled labourers, who were the last to share in times of affluence and the first to be laid off when peace threatened. They would be lucky to earn 20/- a week; about as much as common cutlers. Skilled cutlers might earn 25/-, but their wages and status were declining by comparison with the skilled engineers and steelworkers, who were worth 40/- and upwards. Skilled workers, office workers and laboratory technicians were the first to benefit from the electric trams, which reached Carbrook in 1899. Fares of 1½d to the City Centre were later reduced to 1d, and as the routes extended speculative builders lined them with houses superior to anything in the valley. It was practicable to move to Firth Park, out of the worst of the smoke, with refinements like bay windows, railings at the front and a small garden at the back.

Slum clearance was now a topic being much aired, but the East End was certainly not a priority. The Town Council's first scheme had involved the notorious Crofts District, and it was Carbrook which received the benefit of the notorious Crofts inhabitants displaced by the scheme; new Corporation flats were not for the likes of them. Witnesses from the respectable parts of Carbrook recollected the newcomers tearing up cellar grates for use in gang fights. Certain Crofts ladies became the stuff of legend; in their plush overcoats, which they wore when they meant business, they would use their brollies to see off bailiffs or scramble over the school wall to chastize the headmaster at Coleridge Road.

This typical reaction to newcomers reveals that Carbrook, barely thirty years old, now regarded itself as an established community, with certain families held in respect for the length of their residence. The evidence

Figure 30. Triumphal arch raised by Firth's across Savile Street East at the foot of Carwood Road to welcome Edward VII and Queen Alexandra in 1905. The arch is appropriately made up of warlike products from the Norfolk Works, which can be identified by the helpful labels. Note the drapery designed to draw back and disguise the function of the 'Iron Man' on the left.

collected by Cheryl Parsons and others shows that this new settlement absorbed many traditional Sheffield habits. The local 'feasts' held in summer at Attercliffe, Grimesthorpe, Darnall and Tinsley continued to be observed, at least by the children, and were tending to spread over the rest of the week. Doncaster race days were also general holidays, with the adults commandeering every conveyance and children lining the route in the hope of being thrown fruit or 'Bunny-o'. As late as 1873 the American vice-counsel reported that 'in the great steelworks of Sheffield… scarcely any work is done on Monday and very little on Tuesday'. This was principally in honour of the traditional 'Saint Monday' holiday, but the opportunity was also taken for repairs. After 1870 compulsory education began a slow war of attrition against such distractions, and removed the younger boys from their fathers' sides in the works. In Carbrook, the 1870 Act was often seen as foisting education on families who felt their children could be more profitably employed elsewhere. The Church of England had established a National School on Carbrook Street in obvious anticipation of the far more imposing building which the School Board put up on Attercliffe Common. Their philosophies were very different. The Board School would make no concessions to accommodate the practice of older girls delivering lunches to their fathers and elder brothers at their works by 12.30. It did, on the other hand, establish an enviable academic record. The National School tried an opposite approach. The headmaster, Edgar Wolstenholme, developed a remarkable empathy with the local community. He ensured that 'Natch' pupils got free meals in hard times, that they were first in the queue for Councillor Kelley's monster Christmas bags, and that a disproportionate number qualified for trips into the countryside. Several East End schools were fortunate in their headmasters. Mr Dawn at Coleridge Road turned the ex-Crofts mob into a champion choir whose performances on tour (with supporters' club) inspired respect from the whole region. Mr Wells was to work similar wonders with the Brightside School Football Team. These activities were to some extent in competition with events organized by almost every Church and Chapel in the district.

One of the notable features of the period is the number of sporting and social activities organized by the works themselves for workers and families. One of the earliest of these sponsorships was the annual floral and horticultural show for Sandersons' employees which started in 1859. There were outings, fishing clubs, brass bands and orchestras. Hadfields Sports Dramatic and Operatic Society and the Atlas and Norfolk Football Club are just two famous names, the football club being founded by Jim Clark, melting manager at Firth's who had been goalkeeper for Wednesday. Several works had sports grounds, sometimes well away from the East End. Jonas and Colver's at Millhouses was rather an extreme example; for families who could not afford the tram fare it was a good Sunday walk.

The dominant impression from reminiscences of East End residents is of very little money to spare. The only resident middle-class families were larger shopkeepers and doctors. Some of these were remembered as aloof and lonely figures, though records show that there were many dedicated medical men, from the colourful anarchist Dr Creaghe who never charged working class patients—and never paid any rent—to others who gave up their free time to organizing ambulance classes in the works. Many people preferred to consult housewives who prescribed home remedies and other housewives made a little money by buying basic foodstuffs from the larger shops and reselling in very small portions. Curiously the Brightside and Carbrook Co-op, founded in 1867 and the earliest in Sheffield, soon become quite as unwelcoming as the large Attercliffe stores, with a complicated system of chits and stamps dispensed as if they were charity. Charity was of course unacceptable and children caught begging would be punished. 'Breadlefting' outside the works or collecting 'jubilee' (coagulated coal dust) from the canal side were permissible in times of hardship.

Francis Huntsman died in 1879 at the age of 95, forty years after he had ceased to reside in Attercliffe. He had combined moderate paternalism with complete intransigence towards trades unions. The new generation at Tinsley Park honoured the latter tradition; their steel works, removed to Coleridge Road, now played a minor role to the collieries. The 1893

Figure 31. Ambulance team at Howell and Co.'s Tube Works, Alsing Road, in the 1900s. Such teams were sponsored by East End firms from 1890 onwards, using skills their employees had acquired from the armed services or St John's Brigade. Local GPs acted as visiting lecturers and judged the competitions. Doctors Collier, Branson, Selby and Innes Smith are remembered in this connection.

colliers' lock-out seemed set to be a re-run of 1868, but this time it was not imported blackleg labourers who provided the excuse for rioting at Broughton Lane, but a train of blackleg coal which had arrived from Durham. The Yorkshire Miners' Association called mass meetings at Darnall to calm tempers down. Sheffield Collieries were in the mood to settle, but Huntsman's held out to the bitter end. In 1905 a newspaper described Tinsley Park as a basically eighteenth-century complex of small, shallow pits linked by an ancient horse tramway which took the coal to the canal. New deep pits were already being sunk and new coke ovens and comprehensive rail access transformed operations. Some relatively palatial miners' houses appeared on Ranskill Road, off Shepcote Lane, but the community remained an isolated one.

Meanwhile, Attercliffe was developing into a place where money could be readily spent. The Town Council had done its part with baths in 1879

Figure 32. Impromptu open-air service in the East End. The Minister at the harmonium appears to be the Rev. J.E. Reilley, MC, who was in charge of the Attercliffe Wesleyan Mission from September 1928 until his death in a road accident just over a year later. Attercliffe was frequently treated to religious demonstrations during the 1920s. In 1925 the Wesleyans had come into conflict with the followers of the Rev. Pickering, 'Padre of the Unemployed'.

and a public library in 1887. The Library was free, but the baths cost 1d and you had to have or hire a bathing dress. There are many stories of East End lads walking to Endcliffe to save the money. The canal was a nearer alternative, though you could in theory be fined for bathing in its murky waters. Banks arose on High Street of almost urban size and sophistication, and there were branches of Boots and other major stores. Attercliffe's especial boast was a choice of two music halls. The People's Theatre, later the Theatre Royal, opened on Pinfold Lane (later Staniforth Road) in 1897, to be followed a year later by the Alhambra on High Street, destined to acquire wider fame as the Palace. Both theatres included films in their programmes, but Attercliffe progressed early into purpose built cinemas, with the Globe in 1913 and the Pavilion on Attercliffe Common in 1915.

Figure 33. The south side of Attercliffe High Street showing the rather uninspiring exterior of the famous Attercliffe Palace. The photograph was taken some time between 1904, when the building ceased to be the Alhambra, and its first spell as a full-time cinema, which started in 1909.

The historian had much to regret in the early nineteen hundreds. On Oakes Green the supposed pre-Reformation Chapel was one of the buildings swept away. The oak frame of a house on Darnall Road proved so strong that it had to be pulled apart by two traction engines. Attercliffe House, having briefly provided a stately home for the Working Men's Club, was demolished for extensions to the rejuvenated Brown Bayley's. The greatest loss to industrial archaeology was the original Huntsman's Works on Worksop Road. The site was redeveloped for housing, a small compensation for the streets being devoured for Brown Bayleys' extensions across the road.

The feature still notably lacking in the East End was public open space. Private athletic grounds were attached to the Pheasant Inn at Carbrook and there were recreation grounds at Carlisle Street, Bacon Lane and Carbrook, the last provided in celebration of Victoria's Jubilee in 1887. The Carbrook ground was officially upgraded to a Park and was virtually the only place in the East End where trees and flowers could be seen. Carlisle Street lacked even grass, and private gardens were rare. It was said there were only two colours to be seen in Attercliffe, grey and black.

In other respects the East End was not a bad place to live. In comparison with areas in the City Centre housing density was low and so was mortality. Statistics taken during the First World War from the 25 subdistricts within the Borough—including the most affluent suburbs—show that in terms of mortality the two which made up Attercliffe ranked only eighth and thirteenth. Patrick Abercrombie's Civic survey, commissioned by the City Council in 1924, found the concentration of heavy industry in the East End entirely appropriate. He criticised the 'mistaken policy' of allowing homes to take up large tracts of land suitable for heavy industry and foresaw that they would sooner or later have to make way for works extensions.

The outbreak of the First World War was the event for which the East End had been preparing. All the large works did very well on

Figure 34. Attercliffe Road about 1905, with a string of early covered-topped tramcars approaching the Staniforth Road junction from the Sheffield direction. Shipman and Co.'s Attercliffe Steel and Wire Works are on the left. A Corporation dustcart and a butchers' delivery cart are on their way home. It is to be hoped that the horses are looking where they are going.

armaments, and Brown Bayley's entered the new field of special aircraft steel. In 1915 the Ministry of Munitions technically took control of the larger works to co-ordinate supplies and labour and control wages and prices; in practice the old management remained in place. There had initially been a rush among the younger workers to join the armed forces, often encouraged by enthusiastic patriots like Robert Hadfield and, ironically in view of his family origins, Charles Kayser. Skilled steelwork became a reserved occupation, while the ranks of the semi-skilled were supplied by women or youths. This brought women for the first time into the large works in any numbers. Many replacement workers, male and female, were brought in from country districts and housed in hastily constructed 'munitions huts' at Petre Street, Tyler Street and Tinsley Park. These recruits created tensions in the works, as the skilled men feared, not without justification, that they were part of a plot to reduce the standards of skill and, more importantly, their own earning power. By 1916 there was, strangely enough, a marked pacifist tendency in the larger works which found expression in the informal shop stewards' movement. The movement's spokesman was J.T. Murphy, who had workers' control as his aim, which after the Russian Revolution seemed not unrealizable. Its great success in Sheffield had already been demonstrated in 1916, when 10,000 skilled munition workers came out on strike on behalf of a fitter who had been conscripted. He was released in two days.

Figure 35. Lizzie the elephant was requisitioned from a circus to help out in the First World War, releasing horses for service on the Front. She became an integral member of T.A. Ward's establishment at the Albion Works, Savile Street.

Electric arc furnaces were generally introduced during the war; Sheffield had by then adapted a home-made version. Some minor changes took place. Seebohm and Dieckstahl of the Wicker changed its name to Balfour

Darwin and opened a new works on Broughton Road. Sir Joseph Jonas fell foul of anti-German hysteria in 1918 and was convicted of having had 'criminal correspondence' with Germany a year before the war started, an injustice from which neither he nor his firm fully recovered. A solitary Zeppelin made it as far as the East End on 26 September 1916 and managed to release 36 bombs. They did no significant damage to the war effort, but wrecked a chapel in Attercliffe and killed 29 civilians, mostly in Burngreave. As with men, the war produced a severe shortage of horses, and unlikely beasts were requisitioned from circuses to draw heavy castings between the works; the camels did not last long but T.W. Ward's elephant Lizzie is well remembered. By the end of the war Vickers had 11,000 employees and were paying their shareholders a dividend of 12$^1/_2$ per cent. Hadfields were probably even larger and paid 20 per cent.

Figure 36. Cammells' shell shop towards the end of the First World War, as seen by the Ministry of Munitions' official artist. A scene of cheerful bustle in spotless surroundings; the only male in sight is a supervisor sorting out a technical problem.

After the war the King came to the East End to thank the works for their efforts. The euphoria was short-lived as the demand for armaments vanished and the general recession set in. The shop stewards abandoned ambitions of workers' control and concentrated on a struggle to maintain minimum wages. Two household names lost their independence; Jessop Saville was bought by BSA and the bankrupt Jonas and Colver became the only East End outpost of Stuart Goodwin's Neepsend Group. Some firms found salvation in the expanding motor vehicle and aircraft industries. Edgar Allen were progressive as ever, introducing induction melting in 1927 for 'Stag Major' super high speed steel used for cutting tools. Induction melting, which was economical for small melts, was the final blow to the traditional crucible team. New markets had to be found in place of Germany, France, Russia and the United States—now effectively closed—and new steels were needed to compete with Krupp's cemented carbide and America's molybdenum high speed steels.

This was very difficult, and by 1931 employment in the heavy trades in Sheffield had dropped to 47,000 from 66,000 in 1921. Much of the resulting unemployment had to be borne by the East End. Particularly hard hit were returning ex-servicemen and school leavers, as apprenticeships were no longer available.

Sir Robert Hadfield struggled doggedly to keep his firm independent. He resolutely kept up the armour plate capacity at East Hecla, though his only significant customer was, ominously, Japan. Some of his efforts to find other markets were failures; Bean Cars, which Hadfields took over in 1926, went bankrupt in 1931. The Millspaugh plant for paper making machinery which he installed at East Hecla was more successful. The now elderly Sir Robert continued to run the firm autocratically from London or the south of France.

The great innovation of the period was stainless steel, the almost accidental discovery by Harry Brearley at Firth's Laboratory in 1913. Once again there was some delay in finding a practical application for the inven-

Figure 37. John Brown and Co., armour treatment shop, Atlas Works, 1924.

Figure 38. John Brown and Co., hardening an armour plate, Atlas Works, 1924.

Figure 39. John Brown and Co., 6000 ton forging press, Atlas Works, 1924.

tion, and further delays arose out of disputes over patent rights. In the event Brearley went to Brown Bayley's, while Firth's marketed the material for cutlery. The real breakthrough came when Firth's exchanged their expertise in stainless bar, forgings and castings with Krupp's in rolling. Out of this information W.H. Hatfield at the Brown-Firth Laboratories on Princess Street developed 'Staybright', a material which found its way into almost every household, thanks to such promotions as 'Staybright City' at the Ideal Homes Exhibition. Hadfields and other firms took up the discovery.

Post-war trading conditions forced restructuring on the largest firms. The first great merger, United Steel, did not directly effect Sheffield's East End. In 1928 Vickers' and Cammell's remaining interests amalgamated. Rationalization meant concentrating production which was then distributed among plants which had expanded on an ad hoc basis during the war. It could have meant total removal to a virgin site near the coast, but in the event there was no money for such a radical solution, and the East End profited at the expense of Penistone and Openshaw. Cammell's Grimesthorpe Works and River Don were retained and modernized; East Cyclops was closed but later transferred to Firth Brown. Firth's and John Brown's, who had worked in close association since 1902, formally amalgamated in 1930. To Firth's expertise in stainless steel Brown's contributed their own case hardened Nitralloy steel and facilities for heavy forgings. Together they commissioned a new 30-ton electric arc furnace. In 1934 a cross-partnership between Vickers' and Cammell's English Steel Corporation and Firth Brown produced Firth Vickers Stainless Steel, who built a new works on Weedon Street and took over the vacant East Cyclops.

The people of the East End had been hard hit by the recession. Communists were elected to the Board of Guardians and vied with Labour as champions of the unemployed against the restrictive rules on relief. The Rev. T.E. Pickering, padre of the unemployed, was a familiar speaker addressing crowds outside Attercliffe Baths. Rather pathetic troupes of unemployed or ex-service minstrels performed on the Common for a few

Figure 40. The Edgar Allen Football Team who won the first Tinsley Charity Cup, 1920. Mr Richards, on the right, was responsible for sponsorship of sports within the Imperial Works. The 'Edgar Allen Works and Sports Magazine' of the inter-war years gave details of several football and cricket teams as well as chess, photographic, angling and gardening competitions, all sponsored by the firm.

pennies. Also associated with unemployment were pitch–and–toss rings, which operated on any piece of derelict land and faded away whenever police appeared. In Sheffield, at least, wherever there were rings there were protection rackets, and one of the most notorious gang exploits occurred on Princess Street in 1925, where William Plommer was stabbed to death outside his house in a brawl. The two Fowler brothers, members of the Alfred Road Gang, were convicted and executed for the offence.

By 1930 there were signs of new investment in the East End. Montague Burton built new premises on Staniforth Road corner in fashionable white faience, with the Astoria Ballroom on the top floor. John Banner, whose family had been established several generations in Attercliffe, built a new department store of the same material in 1933. It was the first store in Sheffield with a moving staircase and displayed extraordinary confidence in the commercial future of Attercliffe. Woolworths and Littlewoods were also represented. The Adelphi, largest and most imposing of Attercliffe's Cinemas, opened in 1920. The Palace, which alternated between theatre and cinema, entered a cinema phase in 1930, its walls embellished with atmospheric murals of Indian or Arabian scenes, only to revert again to a theatre in 1937. The Theatre Royal had by this time decided to become a cinema. Works continued to foster a full social life, and school treats, trips and May Day celebrations displayed much variety. It seems that Chapel and Church life was weakening, especially among the young. Dingy premises and lantern slides were no match for the Astoria Ballroom or the Adelphi, and chapel elders were moving out of the district and out of tune with 1930s' youth. Nevertheless it was still possible for a clergyman like the Methodist Rev. Reilley, who had endeared himself to the East End by touring the streets with his portable harmonium, to earn great respect, as the crowds at his funeral in 1929 attested.

Labour's accession to power in the City Council in 1926 had little immediate impact on the East End. Those making reasonable wages had the opportunity of applying for a Council house on one of the new estates to the north. Most of the East-enders stayed where they were. Some of the

Figure 41. Hadfields, like their next door neighbours Edgar Allen, were keen promoters of sports and recreational activities for employees and their families. Their Dramatic and Operatic Section were notable, and in 1926 performed Gilbert and Sullivan at the Attercliffe Palace. In the 1930s they produced spectacular musical comedies at the City Hall.

Carbrook Board School children won scholarships for the Central School, but very few actually made it to secondary education. Family poverty was the main reason; those who overcame this obstacle faced a long tram journey to the Central School or to grammar schools in distant middle-class suburbs.

1935 saw the start of the National Defence Programme and the reinvigoration of the East End. The English Steel Corporation's investment was justified and further new plant was financed by the Government.

Figure 42. Attercliffe Road, looking towards Banners', 1948, showing the shopping centre redeveloped during the 1930s. The centre drew shoppers from all the northern and eastern suburbs, though crossing the busy main road clearly presented a hazard. Banners' new store, completed in 1934, was noted for its escalators and the overhead system which delivered your change, which in Banners' case usually arrived in the form of tokens.

Hadfields' underemployed armour plate mills had to be augmented. But it was not quite like the build-up to 1914, in that firms were no longer free to expand as they chose. It was now deliberate policy to disperse new development away from the East End to lessen the impact of a major bombing raid.

When the Second World War broke out the nation was dependent on the River Don's 15-ton steam hammer for drop forging crankshafts for Spitfire engines. Hadfields were the only firm capable of producing bullet-proof rivets. The Sheffield steel laboratories came into their own. Dr W.H. Hatfield was appointed technical co-ordinator of the Aircraft Alloy Steel Emergency Committee. Their work included analysing steel from captured enemy equipment, as well as developing new steels for the aircraft industry, notably heat-resisting steels for jet engine parts. The English Steel Corporation was involved in the development and eventual production of the giant 'Tall Boy' and 'Grand Slam' bombs. In other cases it was a matter of adaptation; Edgar Allen cast their manganese steel into helmets, Firth Brown used its railway tire forges to make rings for gun barrels and tank turrets, Metrovik at the Tinsley end of Carbrook turned from electric traction equipment to aircraft generators. Spear and Jackson's slogan was 'Saws into Armour', in their case light plating for cars and planes. Other warlike products of the East End included shells, torpedo parts, heavy armour plating and crankshafts for battleships; River Don offered a service of reconditioning crankshafts damaged by enemy mines. Edgar Allens and Jessop's among others produced castings for the Mulberry Harbours needed for the invasion of Europe.

The war machine needed to be kept serviced by huge quantities of ordinary machine tools and tool steel firms like Osborn's and Sanderson Bros. and Newbould's were kept very busy with their traditional lines. Sanderson's even had to re-open their crucible shop in Darnall Road as a stop-gap measure. It was also Sanderson's who received the small but prestigious contract for the Stalingrad Sword.

Evacuation of school children into country districts was planned before the outbreak of war. Most of the East End children went to Leicestershire, which they did not like, and were back home before the Blitz arrived. For most of the East End, the only serious bombing took place on Sunday 15 December 1940. Fog had shielded the valley from very destructive raids during the previous week. Loss of life was largely confined to the east of the area, with incendiary bombs doing much damage. In Coleford Road, ten people were killed by a direct hit on a warden's post. Many people in the area were made homeless as blasts raked through whole terraces. Christ Church itself was burnt out, never to be rebuilt. The principal industrial casualty was Brown Bayley's where four melting shops were put out of action by a single bomb. Damage there was not fully repaired for 15 months. Firth Brown and Metrovik suffered from their roofs being blown off; until they were repaired there could be no working at night for fear that constant flares would alert enemy aircraft. Blackout was a particular problem with the fiery furnaces of the East End. This consideration is said to have been a factor in the closure of the coke ovens at Tinsley Park. The abandonment of Tinsley Park during the war and of Nunnery Pit immediately afterwards marked the end of traditional underground coal working in the East End.

The war drew distinguished visitors to the East End. The King and Queen, Gracie Fields and Winston Churchill all did their bit to raise morale. As before, many women were directed to work in the shell shops and entered new trades such as crane driving for the first time.

In 1945 the City published ambitious plans to rebuild Sheffield. The 1947 planning legislation gave new powers to local authorities. They assumed, correctly in the short run, that the demand for steel would be boosted by postwar reconstruction, particularly as the main European competitors had been laid low. From the point of view of the City Council, it made admirable sense to concentrate heavy industry in the East End to the eventual exclusion of housing, but their only control over industry was a negative one. The post-war governments had their own

Figure 43. In the Second World War women were again drafted into the works to cope with the national emergency. Here in Firth's machine shop the fall of Hitler is being suitably celebrated in May 1945.

agenda for steel, a constant theme being the need to hold prices to aid shipbuilding and the motor vehicle industry. This did not encourage investment or modernization. In 1949 the largest firms, Brown Bayley's, the English Steel Corporation (ESC), Firth Brown's and Hadfields were nationalized, while other famous names, notably Arthur Lee and Samuel Osborn, remained in family hands. The popular view of this period, when prices were fixed and customers so desperate for steel that they were willing to wait years for delivery, is of complacency, but the charge is not a fair one. Within ESC, the River Don Works became the national leaders in forgings for turbo generators, pressure vessels for the nuclear power industry and equipment for offshore drilling rigs. Samuel Fox of Stocksbridge and Firth Vickers jointly set up a rolling mill at Shepcote Lane for mass production of stainless steel, importing a Sendzimir mill from the United States. The English Steel Corporation also had plans for developing the old Tinsley Park Colliery site, originally to produce giant monoblocs of 250 tons or more for power generating plants. The plans were altered, and when they opened in 1963 the works produced billets and bars for the motor industry. The steel was produced by electric arc furnaces, and power vacuum de-gassing was introduced for the first time. It laid claim to be the most modern plant in the country, but the investment had been placed on the unwise assumption that the British motor vehicle industry would continue growing for the indefinite future.

Arthur Lee, a firm which successfully avoided nationalization in 1949, installed its own Sendzimir mill for stainless steel strip in 1948, when Firth Vickers were still having to roll by hand, a process demanding great skill and strength. Lee's employed 2700 by 1962. By 1955 the remaining nationalized firms were back in the private sector, and the boom continued.

A big investor in the area was British Rail. Sheffield's East End was the most concentrated generator of freight business in the country. Following completion of the electric line to Manchester in 1954, British Rail decided to replace their existing goods yards with a huge modern yard built on the old Sheffield District Railway near Tinsley. This involved new approach links from the former South Yorkshire Railway at Carbrook, and the alteration of the Canal to obtain necessary clearance for vessels. Ironically, as far as the East End was concerned, the Sheffield Canal was now irrelevant, and the last commercial traffic to the Sheffield Basin ceased in 1970. Meanwhile, in 1960 the last Sheffield trams made their final journey to Carbrook, where they were broken up in T.W. Ward's scrapyard. The closing of Wicker and Attercliffe Goods Yards potentially released a lot of land, though some of the trackwork was retained for access to private works.

Slum clearance hardly affected the East End before 1970, apart from a few small pockets of back-to-backs. In 1955 a social survey of the Attercliffe area revealed that there were still twenty places of worship in the area and 47 pubs. The pubs were divided into a group of larger premises on the main road, usually faced with glazed yellow bricks (garish but easy to clean), and small pubs on side roads which served the works. The main road group included seven with concert lounges; none had gardens. The survey was pleased to find that Attercliffe was completely free of the 'mean street-corner pubs' which were a feature of the poorer parts of Sheffield. Nearly all the grocers had off-licences, so that every counter displayed bottles of beer and stout among the bread, groceries and vegetables. The young had a choice of ten youth clubs. The boys who frequented them were mostly apprentices, laboratory assistants, clerks and engineers, the girls a 'happy crowd' of shop assistants and factory hands. They started the day well with a fried breakfast, and works' canteens or British restaurants kept them amply supplied during working hours. There was one park, three recreation grounds with cinder tracks, four cinemas, billiard saloons above

Figure 44. Bright Street, 1966, cut in half by the latest extensions to the River Don Works, which had already engulfed substantial areas of residential Carbrook. The terrace houses on the right are clearly superior to their neighbours across the street; they all have front gardens and at the far end also run to bay windows, and in fact boasted kitchen extensions into their back yards. What remains of Bright Street has now been renamed Carbrook Hall Road.

Boots and one of the two Burtons and a skating rink on Church Lane. And of course there was still the Palace, living on its traditions as a venue for top-class variety acts but earning its keep with nude shows. These came to an end in 1955. By all accounts Attercliffe people thought of themselves as a closely-knit working class community and were rather proud of their tough reputation in the rest of Sheffield. Former members, now widely scattered, still recognize each other by their distinctive accent.

The 1950s' boom in special steels once again produced a labour short-age, and for the first time attracted large numbers of workers from over-seas, particularly people who had been born in East or West Pakistan. They arrived usually without their families and took unskilled jobs in the private sector. There were few opportunities for promotion or training. Most of them had no intention of staying permanently. By the early 1970s unskilled jobs were the first to be affected by the end of the steel boom and areas which had provided alternative employment, as in the West Riding textile mills, were also declining. At the same time housing was cheap, as it was now only a matter of time before Attercliffe and Carbrook came under the

Figure 45. The Pavilion Cinema, Attercliffe Common, opened in 1915 with boxes and an orchestra and seats for 1250 people. It was a long time dying. After 1963 it subsisted on a tenuous fare of children's Saturday matinees until 1970 when it appeared to succumb totally to bingo. The local Asian community then stepped in, giving it a new lease of life showing films in Urdu, as when this photo was taken in 1976. The cinema was finally demolished in 1982.

slum clearance programme. So wives and children joined their menfolk and infused a new life in the eastern part of the district with their shops and restaurants in the last few years before its clearance. Traditional Attercliffe was on its way to distant estates like Jordanthorpe, leaving the empty shells of pubs, chapels and cinemas. The new community had no use for pubs or chapels, but prolonged the life of the Pavilion Cinema as a venue for Asian films.

In 1967 steel was renationalized, but only the largest producers, measured by tonnage, were effected. In the Sheffield region, this meant the former United Steel and British Steel Corporation Groups. Rationalization was the order of the day, and the two groups fought each other for survival. In 1972 an agreement was reached under which the stainless steel works at Shepcote Lane was to be modernized at the expense of the River Don Works, which lost its profitable business in small forgings. Sheepcote Lane got continuous casting, but the Tinsley Park works of ESC, brand new in 1963, was closed and dismantled in favour of Stocksbridge. In the private sector, bankers appeared to be taking over and some short-lived mergers took place. Dunford Hadfield, for example, embraced Osborn's, Brown Bayley's and Hadfields. An inevitable accompaniment of every merger was a loss of jobs.

The problem for Sheffield steel was that the increasing sophistication of foreign and third world competition, and the collapse of the home market in engineering, meant that Sheffield had to go for ever higher quality and increased specialization, but at the same time had to produce in sufficient bulk to reduce labour costs and justify investment. In 1980 the British Steel Corporation saw a solution in a series of joint ventures with the private sector which they called 'Phoenix'. Radical thinking was combined with a brutalist management style, which aroused wide hostility in Sheffield. Sheffield Forgemasters slowly and painfully emerged from Phoenix II after 1982. The capacity of the River Don Works for huge forgings was increased, but the last part of John Brown's Atlas Works closed in 1983. It had been modernized only ten years before. Lonrho, owners of Dunford

Hadfield, closed Brown Bayley's and Hadfields' East Hecla Works in the same year.

The major impact of these developments on jobs was not felt until the late 1970s, except among the unskilled. By this time there was little housing left in the East End. Skilled steel workers had moved out into more pleasant suburbs many years before, though they might well continue to use the East End pubs. The housing was not replaced and as no expansion of the works took place, empty spaces were left. A gypsy colony, trading in scrap, became a feature of Attercliffe Common. So the East End escaped the high rise fashion; when slum clearance moved on towards neighbouring Darnall the people were rehoused in the same area on new low-rise developments. The East End was in many ways a more pleasant place to live; the Clean Air Acts and cleaner steel making technologies brought greenery back to the area for the first time in nearly a century. The Canal towpath was converted to a pleasant walk and buddleia sprouted on the River Don Works.

In just over a hundred years the East End had evolved from a classic result of *laissez faire* to the results of too many uncoordinated or contradictory plans. Planning in the steel industry had resulted in dispersing the remaining centres of activity, so that Stocksbridge, Templeborough or Killamarsh were as much part of Sheffield steel as the traditional East End. The City Council had effectively planned away the communities of Brightside and Carbrook but the steel works had failed to move in and fill the gaps. The Government's main contribution to the infrastructure, the M1 motorway, straddled the lower end of the valley. It was a good deal handier for Sheffield than the North Midland Railway had been in 1840. In the 1960s there was nevertheless official unease in the City that the stranger's first view of Sheffield should be quite so uncompromisingly industrial; there was nothing picturesque about East Hecla Works but the name. By 1985 East Hecla was gone, and the view from the viaduct was no longer of the grim sheds of heavy industry but of desolate acres of dereliction.

Acknowledgments

The literature on the East End since 1850 is extensive and anyone requiring further reading will be well rewarded by a visit to the Local Studies Library in the Central Library at Surrey Street. For information on industrial developments I have been particularly indebted to Geoffrey Tweedale's *Steel City* (1986). Cheryl Parsons' *Schools in an Urban Community: A Study of Carbrook* (1987) and Andrew Walker's 1989 Sheffield MA Thesis 'Attercliffe 1841–1881' have also proved particularly useful.

The History of the Lower Don Valley: 1988–1997

Martin Liddament

The early 1980s' recession tore through the fabric of the Lower Don Valley like a whirlwind, destroying jobs, factories and Sheffield's sense of pride in the achievements and traditions of its industrial heartland.

The city reeled from the staggering impact on its workforce. Had the national economic situation not been so dire then the newspaper headlines might have cried out loud and long about job losses and the annihilation of famous companies with histories stretching back to Victorian times.

Sheffield had too many jobs tied to just one industry: metals manufacture. Like a stack of dominoes toppling over, factory closures followed one another in rapid succession, each adding to the human scale of the collapse. Sheffield people watched stunned as the grim but inevitable disintegration of the old industrial order galloped on, followed by the emergence of considerably slimmed-down businesses in which the lucky few still had jobs. By the mid 1980s thousands had been absorbed into the grey pool of anonymity that comes with unemployment. They had been transformed into statistics and relegated to yesterday's news.

Those statistics make grim reading. Between 1975 and 1988 the Valley suffered a reduction in employment from 40,000 to 13,000 jobs. By 1988 fewer than 300 residents remained and 40 per cent of all the available land was vacant, derelict or underused.

If people wearily shrugged their shoulders and accepted job losses as a fact of life, then they could hardly have been expected to get excited about the physical destruction of the old buildings in the Lower Don Valley. Factories, after all, are simply shells. They may be animated by the products that leave their doors and the people who work within their walls, but at the end of the day they are just so much brick and stone.

So a tired and resigned Sheffield watched as huge gaps opened up in their once-great Valley. Firth Brown's works were torn down, leaving two large rectangular scars littered with rubble, twisted metal and the carcasses of the great sheds. Hadfield's was flattened, reducing the narrow brick canyons of Vulcan Road and Weedon Street to a featureless expanse of grey soil, and the remains of the Brown Bailey factory—almost the size of a small village—were scraped out of the Valley by an army of diggers and bulldozers.

As the destruction continued, the city seemed to deny or ignore the remaining industry that still thundered away in isolated pockets of activity. This attitude perhaps reflected a wider national disenchantment with manufacturing. It was the mid 1980s and those people who actually *made* things were seemingly rated second to those who manipulated information and money for a living. As a result it was tempting for Sheffield to look away from its East End, setting its sights instead on the promise of jobs in services or the public sector and viewing manufacturing almost as an irrelevance.

Figure 46. The head office of Thomas Jessop & Co. Broken windows and boarded doors—the legacy of recession in Sheffield.

Neglected, the Lower Don Valley spiralled down a fast track towards complete failure. Problems piled up as the legacy of dereliction and decay triggered increasingly negative feelings among developers and investors and diverted new building work away into other areas, ushering in a period when Valley companies operated as islands of activity surrounded by abandoned sites awash with contamination and covered with the shattered remains of the earlier giant factories. One look at these wastelands was enough to send business pioneers scurrying for greener land, and the joke (partly true) was that visitors to the city, driving up the M1 motorway, would look to their left, see Sheffield, and immediately put their foot hard down on the accelerator until they reached Leeds.

This had been one of the most rapid periods of change in the history of the Valley. Accumulated traditions and above all, the long-established sense of community, had been swept aside by economic and social factors well beyond the control of ordinary men and women.

Figure 47. Carlisle Street East

Once again, the area was at the mercy of powerful forces. But this time, they were subtly different from those that had shaped Victorian Sheffield and its industrial powerhouse that had armed the world through two wars and on into the 1950s. True enough, the men of influence in those times had instigated projects that had changed the face of the Lower Don, but it had been a blind, reactive process where land was taken when it was needed and huge, proud factories and works spread across the Valley, expanding as fast as the ambitions and desires of their owners.

More recent times had seen the start of a new trend. The clearance of much of the old housing from the Valley in the late 1960s and early 1970s had been an indication that the East End was now included in a wider view of Sheffield as a city that could, in some way, be deliberately shaped. Those in authority realized they had some limited power to impose a vision on the area that would override the influence of natural geography, the relatively slow movements of workforces and populations, the gradual introduction of new technology and processes, and the dreams of industrialists—all of which had been factors that had played a part in changing the Valley over the past centuries. Timescales could be compressed. Like a speeded-up film, the shape of the Valley, its very character and purpose, could actually be altered as people watched, squeezing massive alterations into a few brief years.

But even this was no match for the huge, overarching forces of economics and the changes in world markets. The removal of housing from the Valley did nothing to stop or divert the slide into dereliction and decay—indeed, it simply left more scars on the battered face of the area.

As if the derelict sites were not blight enough, the Valley was also badly served by a deteriorating infrastructure, the rail links to London were slow, the environment was in a shocking mess, internal roads were third rate and no single body had the responsibility or the funding to sort it all out by acting in a decisive and coherent way.

By 1987, the situation had become so bad that the public and private sectors in the city, putting aside old disagreements and tensions, decided to cooperate in finding a way forward.

In June of that year, management consultants Coopers and Lybrand, working alongside property and development experts Drivers' Jonas, Crouch and Hogg and the then Sheffield City Polytechnic, were asked to prepare a detailed report for the Sheffield Economic Regeneration Committee. The report set out how the economy of the Lower Don Valley could be revitalized and it presented a number of alternatives.

One scheme was to bring private and public sector bodies together to tackle the problem—but they still would have retained their own identities and would have followed their own agendas—not an ideal solution. Another suggestion, and one the authors of the report favoured, was to set up an Urban Development Corporation, or UDC. The concept of UDCs was relatively new—there were schemes in London Docklands, the North-East and Merseyside—but it seemed workable. The government agreed. Sheffield could have a Development Corporation, and with it £50 million of public money with which to regenerate the Lower Don Valley.

There was good reason to believe that a Development Corporation could make a significant difference to the Valley, even working over a short period. The property and development markets were booming, and there seemed no reason why a powerful body with sweeping powers, including authority over planning issues, could not attract new wealth and businesses into the area, riding on the back of the massive wave of optimism that was driving the economic upswing.

The political situation was somewhat different, however. The idea of a Development Corporation was immediately seen as a threat by the City Council which argued strongly that given a similar budget it could do the job itself, and do it with the blessing of the local electorate. In June 1987 the then Leader of the Sheffield City Council, David Blunkett, was quoted in *Regional Development Magazine* saying, 'Of course we are in favour of Urban Development and Regeneration Grants, but not the UDCs. In Sheffield we would welcome the money, but what we would like is a partnership. UDCs are not a partnership. They are an imposition from the centre.'

These objections cut no ice with the government which pointed out that the offer on the table was a substantial one: a cash hand-out of £50 million to Sheffield for the regeneration of 2000 acres of desperately neglected land. But the essential pre-condition was an independent body to oversee that expenditure for a fixed period of seven years and keep it firmly focused on key areas such as buying and reclaiming sites, improving roads, helping existing firms, attracting inward investment and improving the environment. That body was going to be a Development Corporation.

The situation was defused when both sides agreed to a programme of close, practical consultation. The embryo Development Corporation, chaired by local businessman Hugh Sykes, pledged cooperation with the council and the other public and private sector bodies involved in the city's regeneration plans. The Council—which under the leadership of Clive Betts was already moving towards a more positive, pragmatic relationship with Sheffield businesses—dropped its formal opposition to the creation of the Development Corporation and accepted seats on the SDC's board for three councillors: David Skinner and Helen Jackson from the Labour group and David Heslop from the Conservatives. The stage was set for progress.

By December 1988 a handful of staff had been recruited and had moved into the Development Corporation's headquarters on Savile Street East, opposite the site of Firth Brown's old Atlas Works. Don Valley House, the five-storey building that was to be the SDC's home through the last part of the decade and on into the 1990s, was itself in the process of being refurbished and staff had to pick their way over piles of rubble every morning and work with their coats on until proper heating was installed.

Figure 48. The SDC office (interior). SDC staff were recruited from different backgrounds, but they all shared a common purpose.

The people who were recruited to the SDC came from a variety of backgrounds. Some brought with them years of experience in the private sector. Others were civil servants and local government employees, looking for a change of scene and an opportunity to put specialist skills to the test in a dynamic and exciting environment.

One obvious characteristic of the SDC team was that these were men and women with independent minds. They were willing, in many cases, to take the risk of joining an organization with a short life-span, burning old career bridges behind them as they set out to tackle a new project. There was undoubtedly a strong sense of commitment to the regeneration of the area, and a fierce concentration on the task in hand which compensated for the fact that the total number of staff was quite small: just 40 or so people, even when the Development Corporation was at its largest.

The early months of the SDC's life passed by in a rush. News of its formation had spread widely and there was no shortage of potential buyers for land or property. The telephone lines were busy from day one.

This was still a time of overseas investment—particularly from Japan. Several delegations of businessmen visited from that country, and SDC staff found themselves escorting potential buyers round sites that had not even had the weeds removed, never mind the huge piles of rubble, metal and concrete blocks. The approach was very much to let the mechanics of site preparation catch up with any sales that might be made, and so with formal bowing, presentation of newly-printed business cards and polite conversation, the overseas guests were wooed with a vision of how things might be in three years time.

Figure 49. Atlas Works' site.
Never mind the rubble—think of the possibilities!

One stately Japanese industrialist on being shown the Atlas North site stood motionless for a moment in the middle of what resembled a lunar landscape. He turned slowly, taking in the layout of the thirty-acre wilderness and then produced a compass which he carefully studied, orientating himself to the most auspicious directions. Presumably satisfied that no ill luck could befall a company if it built a factory on the land (despite the extremely obvious evidence to the contrary), he smiled at his hosts as if geomancy were a natural part of sealing multi-million pound development deals. But even his confidence and competitive land pricing from the Development Corporation were not enough to push through a sale on that day.

The SDC was not too worried if potential inward investors went elsewhere in those early months. After all, enquiry was following enquiry in rapid succession. Internal discussions within the SDC therefore focused not on how business was to be generated, but rather on whether selling land to owner-occupiers was going to be more profitable than marketing it to developers. In both cases, the assumption was that the Valley would soon fill up with new companies, putting the SDC in the role of a general with a grand strategy and plenty of room to manoeuvre.

There was a belief in the immediacy of the solution that the SDC represented; certainly outside the organization and—possibly because it was so frenetically busy from its inception—inside it as well. 'We have to respond!' could have been the Corporation's motto during that period of its life, 'what's the best we can do in the shortest time?' Because urban regeneration was—and still is—an imprecise discipline, there was no formula that could be applied to tell if the early goals were realistic and no-one could say for sure whether or not the organisation had been set an impossible task.

With the benefit of hindsight, we can see that, as in all things, there was a down side to the situation. High levels of demand were bound to pose significant problems for two reasons: first, the SDC at that time owned absolutely no land out of the 2000 acres it had to regenerate, and secondly, the people who *did* own plots wanted to sit tight and watch the value of their holdings soar as the mere existence of the Development Corporation stimulated the market.

The Corporation had been given a flying start with its substantial budget and what seemed at the time to be a realistic seven-year period in which to work. Its first Chief Executive, Keith Beaumont, was able in October 1988 to point to a number of important schemes: notably the Meadowhall regional shopping and leisure centre and the Canal Basin retail and commercial project which had already attracted a £10.5 million Urban Regeneration Grant. John Hambidge, then Director of the city's Chamber of Commerce also identified these schemes as being of critical importance and added the planned Sheffield Airport and the City Council's World Student Games facilities to a list of 'exciting projects' that he saw lifting Sheffield out of the economic rut. 'The resurgence of confidence in Sheffield is rapid and astonishing, given that this has really only started within the last twelve months', he said. 'Sheffield is now well and truly on the move and going places—fast.'

Keith Beaumont was slightly more cautious. There was a lot to be done on the land ownership side, he told *Regional Development Magazine*.

This was an understatement. Behind the scenes the pressure to buy land and make a start on projects was intense. Throughout its life the SDC's staff were to feel the pressure of time as the days and weeks ticked away. The team knew they would be judged on the number of jobs created and the amount of new steelwork emerging from derelict sites, but the life of the SDC was always going to be very limited in comparison with the long history of the Valley.

It is important to understand just how much power the SDC had. As an Urban Development Corporation it took on all planning authority for the area it covered, which stretched from the old canal basin by the city centre, out along Carlisle Street East and on to junction 34 north on the M1 motorway. Its boundaries then ran south along the M1 and cut back towards the city at Tinsley Park, embracing a large area that contained derelict steelworks, part of the Tinsley Park municipal golf course, and the thriving business of British Steel Stainless (later to become Avesta). From there, the boundary line headed towards Attercliffe, skirting the sites identified as likely homes for the sporting facilities of the World Student Games, eventually running down Attercliffe Road and Savile Street East to end at the Wicker archway. Within this area, the SDC could enforce environmental legislation, compulsorily buy land and buildings, and even ask Parliament to vest land in it.

At the time, it seemed likely that the Development Corporation would certainly need to flex some or all of these legal muscles, and so it was that it embarked on a series of actions that were to colour its early activities and plunge it into controversy.

The first task was relatively innocuous: to find out who actually owned what. The years of neglect in the Valley had left records in a shambles, so teams of property specialists were sent out literally knocking on doors and marking up ownerships on maps. The results confirmed the SDC's fears. Too many key sites were split up—at least on paper—with several individuals or organizations owning a bit here and there. 'Large-scale dereliction demands large-scale solutions,' said the SDC and set about posting notices and sending letters that warned companies that they were within areas that could be included in compulsory purchase order (or CPO) plans aimed at assembling sites that could then be reclaimed and put onto the market.

Another factor driving this decision was the need to improve the road system in the Valley. It was clear from the earlier work of London Docklands Development Corporation that new buildings and regeneration sites need to be fed by modern transport networks in the same way that a growing body needs to be supplied with life blood by its arteries. People must be able to get in and out of an area in order to work, to shop and enjoy leisure activities. Companies have to move goods to and from factories. They have to get them on to motorways or rail links with the minimum delay.

Original designs for the road envisaged a tree-lined boulevard that would run as a wide dual carriageway through the centre of the Valley from the M1 to the Wicker arches. It would have a massive positive impact on journey times and freight movement, while giving an equally important boost to the appearance of the area.

But wide roads need a lot of land. At this stage, no companies had actually been bought out, but the possibility that this might happen sparked fears in businesses of all sizes. Teams of solicitors and commercial agents were mobilized by worried firms and the media embraced the story with enthusiasm, taking up the cases of business people who claimed that the uncertainty caused by the CPO programme was damaging their companies.

The Development Corporation's proposals were certainly wide-ranging. If implemented, the CPO process would have been one of the most complex of its kind ever undertaken in the UK. Staff teams worked round the clock on the plans, helped by consultants brought in from top London firms.

Looking back at this time it is clear that the SDC followed strict legal advice in its approach to the CPOs. Warned by its professional advisors that a set procedure needed to be followed with regard to sending out letters and informing companies of its intentions, the Development Corporation missed the opportunity to actually sit down across the table from the firms involved and talk through its plans and objectives. Worse, it believed that most companies would even be unwilling to smarten up their property without the threat of compulsory purchase hanging over them.

It is easy to see how a 'them and us' attitude sprang up as the two sides became polarized. From the viewpoint of existing companies, the SDC had been imposed from on high, with frightening powers to alter the future of businesses which had only recently struggled out of recession. They wanted help, not more uncertainty and though they agreed that the Valley should become a better place to work, they wanted their own firms to be left alone to get on with what they knew best—making top quality products.

The Development Corporation was moving quickly, it was new, it was staffed mostly by people who did not have their roots in the area. These perceptions only served to feed concerns that a 'big brother' body was looming over the Valley's embattled manufacturers.

By January 1989 the *Financial Times* was reporting on a tense meeting held in the surreal venue of the old Adelphi Cinema in Attercliffe. Representatives of the newly-formed Don Valley Business Association squeezed behind disued bingo desks to hear Hugh Sykes address them from the cinema's old wooden stage. The prize at stake would have raised the Adelphi's rafters had it been a bingo night: an offer of £5 million in grants to help companies refurbish and extend their premises. The members of the Association, which represented more than 100 firms opposed to' the Development Corporation's CPO plans, looked singularly unimpressed. The officers of the SDC knew they had a battle on their hands.

Again, looking back it is now clear that the early vision of a valley swept clear of dereliction and rebuilt in a series of large, high-profile projects was over-optimistic. The scent of success had the pulses of Sheffield's great and good racing, but not enough thought was given to the views and feelings of those companies that had emerged battered and bleeding from the wreckage of the early 1980s.

Questions were soon being asked as to whether regeneration should threaten these firms. In September 1989 the *Star* said 'Hundreds of acres are to be cleared, old buildings razed, new factories, offices, homes and shops built and green areas and riverside walks created'. However, the paper recognized that some 150 firms could be put out of business in the process.

'This upheaval is the price of progress, but Sheffield must ensure that firms now playing an important role in local industry are not lost', said the leader writer under the banner headline 'The New East Enders'.

At the time, some prominent companies were included in the CPO areas. Firms such as the Charles Clark Group on Savile Street, Forgemasters, Marshall's Hard Metals and Thesco Ltd. were all named in lists published by the SDC and printed in the local papers.

In the meantime, other stories were hitting the news pages. The SDC announced that work was starting on the Tinsley park site, preparing it for opencasting. The idea of an airport to be built on the site after the coal had been extracted was once again mooted, and Retford firm A.F. Budge (Mining) Ltd. was named as the winner of the £26.8 million opencasting contract.

The work planned for the site was to sweep away the remains of the huge steelworks that had operated at Tinsley. Its very foundations would be gouged out of the ground by massive earth moving and digging machinery to expose the rich seams of high quality coal that lay beneath.

At the same time, almost unnoticed and unremarked apart from a short article in the *Star*, a relic from another steelworks found a new lease of life. A 25-tonne basket used to feed steel scrap into arc furnaces at Stocksbridge Engineering Steels was donated by the company to the council for incorporation into landscaping surrounding the facilities for the World Student Games; at that time under construction in the city's East End. Converted into a viewing platform, it was to be placed on a mound alongside a grassed area between the athletics stadium and indoor arena. People who climbed up it would have a panoramic view over the Valley—a view which, despite the brave and bold predictions quoted in the media, was showing a depressing tendency to stay grim, grey and unaltered.

By early 1990, the recession was upon the UK. The SDC and its embryonic plans were not immune from it. The first signs in the Lower Don Valley had been the slowing of progress on proposed development schemes such as the mixed office, light industrial and retail project planned for Atlas South—the former site of Firth Brown's works on Savile Street East. Enquiries were still coming in but the companies concerned were not taking them beyond the first stages. It was as though the customers wanted to keep an eye on developments in the Valley, but were unwilling to commit themselves any further.

There was still activity, however. The Development Corporation pressed on with its plans to create the new spine road running through the centre of the Valley, but now it was becoming apparent that the original grand scheme was going to have to be slimmed down. Ideally, the road would, with its generous dimensions and sweeping lines of trees, have had a strong presence all of its own. However, the engineers' reports and consultants' projections were showing that more work than expected would have to be done in order to match the scale of the original vision. The cost would simply be too high.

Alternative proposals were put forward, and eventually it was decided to agree a simpler road scheme that would improve the existing highway and only add a few new sections. It would still be dual carriageway for most of its length, but it would be a more realistic project. Better still, fewer companies than first expected were going to have to be moved to make way for the work.

The big name companies whose inclusion in the CPO areas had caused much shaking of heads and worries that the Development Corporation

Figure 50. Even in 1989 the River Don showed its promise as a green corridor running through the centre of the Valley.

was in danger of throwing away some of the best performing businesses in Sheffield, were now taken out of the compulsory purchase scheme.

This was good news for relations between the SDC and the firms in the Valley, especially as other landowners were now showing signs of being willing to discuss the sale of plots, enabling the SDC to meet its targets of acquiring large sites that would be attractive to developers or companies wanting to build and occupy their own premises—at least when the recession eased.

May 1990 saw another important story emerge: one that was to run and run for the remainder of the Development Corporation's life. At a packed press conference in London, the SDC announced that an airport was to be built at Tinsley Park, putting Sheffield on the international air travel map and giving the city—the largest in Europe without an airport—facilities that would boost its economic revival.

Civil engineering experts A.F. Budge, who were already contracted by British Coal to remove 1.5 million tonnes of coal from the site, were named as the developers of the airport and a 50 acre business park adjacent to its planned 1.2-kilometre runway. When all the costs were added up, it looked as though the scheme would represent a £100 million investment—exactly the sort of private sector deal the Corporation had been seeking and one which would not cost the public purse a single penny.

The airport was scheduled to open in the summer of 1993, with aircraft like the 107-seater BAe 146 expected to use it. From day one, it was intended to be a business airport. No charter flights were planned and it was clear that the geography of the surrounding area would prevent the runway from being lengthened at any time in the future. Sheffield might be getting an airport at last, but it would be a relatively small one, allowing local business people to fly to European and UK destinations, but not capable of taking the large jets needed for transatlantic or other long-haul routes. At the time, Richard Budge, Managing Director of A.F. Budge (Mining) Ltd. admitted that no airlines had expressed a commitment to using the airport and that its success would depend on aggressive marketing. Perhaps some warning signs were there, if people had been able to read the wider economic picture, but at the time the airport plans generated a wave of euphoria amongst the business community and a limited, if vocal, chorus of complaints from nearby residents. Even a public meeting that looked set to turn into a protest against the airport plans petered out into a series of isolated attacks. The airport would be a financial non–runner, said Geoff Deeley, Head of the Tinsley Park Action Group, 'it will create few jobs'. His views were in the minority, at least amongst the wider Sheffield business community.

This was a time of consolidation for the SDC. Despite its slow progress the Corporation remained firm in its conviction that the entire area could be changed by adhering to a grand vision and it looked once again to its strengths as a planning body to draw up a framework of change for the area. Published as a series of maps over the remainder of the SDC's life, this planning framework showed exactly how land could be used; where new roads would go and where fresh landscaping would revitalize tired and visually unrelieved areas. It is perhaps significant that these large, bright visions of a massively altered Valley remained the single most popular publications to emerge from the Development Corporation over the following years.

It seemed that the Development Corporation was shaking off its controversial image and starting to gain a reputation for doing things right at last, although this view was not shared by everyone.

On 25 June 1990, Helen Jackson, then a Board Member of the SDC and Chair of the Council's Employment and Economic Committee, announced she would be resigning from the Development Corporation. Councillor Jackson unleashed a volley of criticisms aimed at the organization on whose Board she had sat for two years. The task of revitalizing the Lower Don Valley had been set back because of the SDC, she claimed 'I don't feel that the SDC has achieved a great deal'.

The criticism stung, particularly as the Corporation felt it had been working hard to put in place the plans and administrative structure needed to get large-scale development under way. True, little physical change had occurred in the Valley, but many land deals had been struck and the Corporation was building up a valuable pool of sites as well as sorting out the extremely complicated legalities of building the new road and securing the airport deal. The SDC responded with restraint, not wanting to enter into a public slanging match that would dent Sheffield's prospects of attracting new business. It was 'amazed' by the remarks, it said. Three hundred acres of land had been acquired, nine sites were being worked on and more than £600,000 given towards improvement schemes.

Five days later, the Corporation had another excellent news story to counter the chilly blast from Helen Jackson. Plans to house a major part of the Royal Armouries collection in a purpose-built Sheffield museum were going to be submitted for government approval. The outline plans involved moving much of the collection from the Tower of London to a site adjacent to the Meadowhall scheme which was itself due to open in the autumn of that year. The whole project seemed sure to bring an economic boost to South Yorkshire and there was talk of millions of visitors coming to see the attraction every year.

Just as things seemed to be going the Development Corporation's way, a major row erupted within the organization.

Like many bodies of its kind, the SDC had been given a role that placed it somewhere between the public and private sectors. Expected to act quickly and decisively, with all the flexibility and imagination of an entrepreneurial company, it still had to work within the carefully thought-out, complex rules and regulations of the public sector which funded it and which enforced the validity of its decisions—especially those involving planning issues.

This dual nature was reflected in its Board structure, which drew on talented, highly individualistic people from both sectors in order to bring the two areas closer together. Of course, this mix could create problems as well as solutions, especially in the intense local atmosphere in which every action of the Corporation was subjected to scrutiny, debate and frequent criticism.

Unfortunately the pressures became too great. Following disagreements between SDC's Chief Executive, Keith Beaumont, and its Chairman, Hugh Sykes, the board decided to seek the early retirement of the Chief Executive; and Mr Beaumont sent a file to the SDC's paymasters, the Department of the Environment, which contained a number of criticisms of Mr Sykes, who was next in line to be Sheffield's Master Cutler. The government set up an inquiry headed by retired civil servant Sir John Garlick, a highly respected figure. With Keith Beaumont on extended leave, the inquiry continued. In July, Graham Kendall, a top civil servant and a director of the Department of Employment's Training Agency, was appointed temporary Chief Executive. The inquiry then ran until the end of August when Michael Portillo, then Inner Cities Minister with the Department of the Environment, announced that no evidence of harm or wrongdoing could be found, that the Chairman had acted with complete honesty and integrity, but that clearer guidelines were needed in the future to prevent similar problems arising within Urban Development Corporations. Keith Beaumont took early retirement, the story died away and the Development Corporation emerged from a period of self-imposed silence to tell the world that it was business as usual—but with a much stronger emphasis on understanding the market and putting more effort into focusing on the needs of different types of customer.

Business was certainly the name of the game at Meadowhall in the north-eastern corner of the Lower Don Valley. Here a huge site, once occupied by steel giants Hadfields, had been transformed into one of the biggest shopping malls in Europe.

Meadowhall's statistics were staggering. Costing £250 million to build, with shopfitting and associated costs piling another £200 million on top

Figure 51. Visions of change—the domes of Meadowhall take shape,
appearing over the walls of a derelict factory.

of that figure, this was the biggest private sector investment to hit Sheffield
for decades. The brainchild of local businessman Paul Sykes and Stadium
Developments' Eddie Healy, Meadowhall was a city within a city—totally
enclosed to give the highest standards of shopping comfort in a carefully
controlled and secure environment. Acres of free car parking—enough for
11,000 vehicles—and plenty of facilities for families added to the attraction of the complex and its 1.2 million square feet of shops. For those
wanting to come by rail there was also a purpose-built station with two
platforms and ultra-modern facilities on the way, plus a promised link into
the forthcoming Supertram rapid light transport system.

In September 1990 the doors opened and a wave of people rushed in. They packed the malls and thronged in the Oasis—a huge food court with a 48-screen video wall and space for thousands of diners. It was American-style shopping come to Sheffield, and the local people loved it. Their feelings were echoed by shoppers from Leeds, Nottingham, Rotherham and Doncaster who flocked to Meadowhall, making predictions of first year visitor figures approaching 25 million people look quite realistic.

The City Council, who originally gave planning permission for the complex, were as proud as anyone. The Development Corporation were delighted to have such a large flagship scheme transforming a key part of the Valley. Once again, Sheffield opinion was carried along on a wave of optimism and few people gave any heed to the lone dissenting voices who worried about the future of an increasingly neglected and abandoned city centre.

Figure 52. The glittering prize—Meadowhall's award-winning malls and public area transformed shopping in South Yorkshire.

Meadowhall was certainly spectacular, but it was not the only story in the Valley. As the threat of widespread compulsory purchases had lifted, so opposition to the Development Corporation started to lessen. There was even time to pursue lighter, environmental issues, such as the thousands of fish that were returned to the River Don as part of a programme to improve the quality of the long-neglected waterway.

The fish—a mix of dace and chub—arrived at the riverside courtesy of Yorkshire Water. The huge plastic bins containing the swirling mass were gently lowered into the water in front of waiting journalists and camera crews. Would the fish survive? Would they flounder in the murky water, which was still far from clean?

To everyone's relief, they swam away and several years later were being caught as mature specimens in perfect condition, much to the delight of local anglers. Few people realized it at the time, but as reports in the media later revealed, the fish had been bred in still water tanks and might have been swept away by the river currents had they not been 'trained' to swim against the flow while still at the farm. 'The National Rivers Authority staff have to put the little fellows through the fishy equivalent of a weight training course before they can trust them to life in the fast lane of the Don', reported the *Star*.

The Valley's other waterway, the canal, also attracted attention. Towards the end of 1990, Graham Kendall, now formally appointed as Chief Executive of the Development Corporation, announced that two new developers had been shortlisted to put forward plans for the ill-fated Cutlers' Wharf site at the city's old canal basin. Property company Shearwater had failed to bring forward a scheme to transform the site into a mix of housing, retail and offices, so other developers including the company Norwest Holst were asked to draw up detailed proposals for the historic 50-acre site.

The canal basin had played an important role in the industrial history of the Lower Don Valley, but it had fallen into a terrible state of disrepair. The historic listed buildings at its core were empty shells and its wharves were piled high with litter and half-repaired boats. The canal itself was choked by toxic silt and rats roamed freely around the water's edge.

Now, with Shearwater's four-year-old scheme abandoned, the new proposals from the shortlisted developers included many more offices and a 150-bed hotel. An art gallery, craft market, filling station and restaurant were also proposed, along with a heritage centre, a design innovation centre and an arena for open-air events.

Further down the Valley, plans were also being put forward for a £60 million 'Chinatown' development on the site of the old Broughton Lane sidings. Proposals had been put to the SDC for a hotel, shops, a conference centre, pagodas, a temple and water garden as well as high-quality offices and homes. Much of it was to be built to traditional Chinese designs, said the developers. At least it made for some good artist's impressions which were printed in the local media and in the property press.

It was now 1991, the year that the World Student Games were destined to come to Sheffield. The Lower Don Valley was the focus of a period of frantic preparation as the City Council, who were responsible for the Games, put the finishing touches to a superb 25,000 seat athletics stadium (already open) and an 11,000 seat indoor arena. In the city centre, the huge Ponds Forge swimming and sports complex neared completion, set to offer the best competition swimming facilities in Europe, if not the world.

The Games themselves were a curious event, aimed at an international audience and designed to provide a platform for young athletes, many of whom would go on to enter Olympic competitions. Several years earlier Sheffield had been told that the Games had been 'won' for the city and that they were second only the Olympics themselves in terms of their size and importance. A world wide audience was guaranteed for Sheffield—or so it seemed at the time.

The truth was somewhat different. The Games had previously been held in a succession of states, many of them in the Communist bloc, and had been heavily subsidized by the governments of the countries concerned. Coverage of the events had never made it as far as the UK and there was no reason why the BBC or ITV should have rushed to grab the broadcast rights for something they perceived to be of relatively low significance. Whether they were right in this view is a matter of opinion, the fact remains that Sheffield had bid for an expensive sporting event that few countries wanted (there was actually no competition from other nations for the staging of the 1991 Games) and for which there was no established television audience. With the UK's major terrestrial broadcasters unwilling to commit air time to the Games' wide-ranging sporting programme, it was virtually impossible to raise sponsorship of the kind needed to offset the enormous cost of staging the event. A contract with British Satellite Broadcasting had raised hopes briefly, but folded when BSB merged with Sky in November 1990.

To be fair, many individuals from the public and private sector gave up their time to try and make the Games a financial success. Hundreds of people worked together for the good of the city to get the Games staged. Old rivalries were put aside and political hatchets buried for the duration. For a while, the city had a common purpose.

Sadly, the economic situation was worsening. It was Dr Paul Foley, a lecturer in employment planning at Sheffield University who summed up the dangers in a paper presented to a conference of the Institute of British Geographers.

'Sheffield's new sporting image could do much to change negative perceptions of the city as a sooty industrial town', said Dr Foley. 'It was hoped a revival in Sheffield's image would encourage more businesses to move to the city. Unfortunately, figures show the rate of industrial movement among businesses is decreasing. Continuation of the current economic slump could well coincide with the Games taking place, making it far more difficult to attract businesses to the city and cash in on Sheffield's new image.'

Dr Foley was right, but despite the economic threat it seemed that everyone was still thinking big.

Norwest Holst won the contract to rebuild the canal basin and pledged to complete the work by the summer of 1994. Up to 2500 jobs were predicted to be on the cards as a result of the work, with 750,000 square feet of floorspace set to be created.

On dry land, the Danish company behind the Legoland theme park at Billund considered the Lower Don valley as a site for a UK spin-off.

Meadowhall's success as a leisure destination had helped this idea take shape, but like many of the schemes proposed around that time, it came to nothing. Even the idea of new 'Tivoli Gardens' to rival those in Copenhagen and built on sites around the Meadowhall complex fizzled out after a few weeks of intense media interest.

Then a bitter blow was dealt to Sheffield. In June 1991 the government announced that the Royal Armouries project was going to go to Leeds. Sheffield was losing out to a carefully co-ordinated bid supported by substantial private sector cash. Leeds businesses had got behind the idea of the Armouries in a big way. A site in the Clarence Dock area of the River Aire was available, close to Leeds railway station and the end of the M1 motorway. The combination of location and financial package had swung the decision in West Yorkshire's favour.

The loss of the Armouries project heralded a lull in activity throughout the Lower Don Valley. For the next six to eight months, development marked time as SDC's team fought to win business in a sluggish market.

Despite the difficulty of progressing individual schemes, the Development Corporation pressed on with its vision, setting out artists' impressions of how different parts of the Valley could eventually look once transformed into new, productive areas set in more attractive, landscaped surroundings. A series of imaginary views drawn from the perspective of drivers using the proposed new road were also produced.

The new year saw the glimmer of hope return. Plans to allow a 200,000-square-feet retail park to be built close to Meadowhall sparked renewed criticism from the City Council, the Chamber of Trade and the Motor Retailers Group. The Development Corporation, by now

Figure 53. The Meadowhall Retail Park—more variety and more controversy.

123

aware that its successes could almost be charted by the rise and fall of these types of attack, continued with the scheme after a study showed it would have a negligible impact on the city centre. In fact, many other towns and cities had similar retail parks and Sheffield was simply catching up with the rest of the market.

Figure 54. Inside the Abbey National building at Carbrook.

In February, another first was announced: Abbey National plc was to bring its Share Registry headquarters to the Lower Don Valley, locating the new business in a 35,000-square-foot building that had been put up by Chesterfield-based developers Glenlivet at the very end of the property boom and was sitting there ready-made for a quality occupier. The site formed part of the Carbrook Hall Business Park and was already home to the City Council's Design and Building Services, housed in 75,000 square feet of modern offices that had already been built by Glenlivet.

Abbey National's Commercial Services Director Geoffrey Osbaldeston said, 'We chose Sheffield because of its excellent facilities, the quality of its labour force and the co-operation we received from the SDC, City Council and developers'.

The significance of this blue-chip move was not overlooked by the media and the Abbey National story made the

major papers as well as the local press and key trade and technical maga-
zines. Suddenly attention was focusing on actual buildings and solid examples of success. The Carbrook Hall Business Park was quoted as an example
of the 'ripple effect'—a wave of confidence and development spreading
outwards from the hugely successful Meadowhall complex to stimulate
activity in the immediate vicinity.

In retrospect, this was a key turning point for the Development
Corporation. The Carbrook area was fast becoming a microcosm of the
Valley as a whole—at least as the SDC saw it. The City Council had already
moved its Design and Building Services Department into 75,000 square
feet of brand new offices behind the Abbey National site, and it looked as
though work on the new road would soon start to improve the transport
links into this important part of the Lower Don.

By now, the SDC could calculate it had helped to create or secure 2000
full-time jobs in the Valley. This was on top of the 4000 created at
Meadowhall and those involved in the Abbey National project. A quarter
of the jobs had come from existing firms that had expanded with the help
of grants from the Development Corporation—grants of up to 50 per cent
of approved costs which could range from just a few hundred pounds to
hundreds of thousands.

Refurbishment schemes were bringing in around £8 of private sector
investment for every £1 spent by the SDC. A map of the Valley published
by the *Star* in February identified thirty-eight projects that might go ahead
during the life of the Corporation; projects with the potential to create
thousands more jobs.

Two schemes which were to have a significant impact on the Valley were
also progressing at that time, more or less out of the public eye. One was
the construction of the Supertram line running from Meadowhall to the
city centre. Snaking up the side of the Valley, following the line of a disused
railway, the Supertram route was part of a £250 million network that
would give Sheffield the UK's first genuine modern road-running tram

system, one that was planned to play a major role in a public transport strategy designed to ease traffic congestion and provide a more environmentally friendly solution to moving people round the area.

The second scheme was hidden away underground. The Don Valley Intercepting Sewer was being built by Sheffield City Council on behalf of Yorkshire Water, and it was a massive engineering project that had already been running for twelve years. The idea was to take the strain off the old nineteenth-century network of drains and sewers which was threatening to become overloaded every time it rained heavily in Sheffield. The Intercepting Sewer was also planned to remove the danger of pollution running into the rivers Don, Loxley, Rivelin, Porter and Sheaf.

Big enough to have a single decker bus driven through its main tunnel, the sewer was designed to serve 440,000 people, extend for over 12 miles and cover an area of 47 square miles. Up to 11,500 gallons could be handled every second, delivering an average daily flow of 38.5 million gallons to the Blackburn Meadows treatment works by the Tinsley Viaduct. It was a prime example of the kind of major infrastructure work that was going on all the time in the Lower Don Valley, unnoticed and unremarked even by the people who travelled through the area every day or who worked there.

April brought in another success for the Development Corporation: a pioneering move by building and civil engineering contractors George Banks Ltd onto the former steelworks site at Atlas North.

The 30-acre site had just been reclaimed to the highest European standards by the Development Corporation in a £4 million clean-up project involving the removal of old concrete foundations, soil contaminated by heavy fuel oils, scrap metal, asbestos and even PCBs, the chemicals used in electrical transformers that had leaked out into the ground when the site was used to break up equipment a few years earlier.

The cost of clearing Atlas North and putting in new roads, landscaping and services was more than the private sector had been willing to pay. It was a vindication of the Development Corporation's strategy of pumping public money into the reclamation of derelict land in order to create jobs and improve the environment. But the project had not been without its problems.

When the first excavators started working on the site their operators soon discovered that the foundations for the old steelworks went down an enormous twenty feet or so. This massive concrete raft had to be chipped away, broken up and crushed to a gravely powder on the site before it could be recycled or removed. This was slow, laborious work, made more difficult by the fact that decades before, some bright spark had tipped a load of artillery shell cases into what would have then been liquid cement, presumably to dispose of them quickly and cheaply. Now, every time a shell was discovered, the bomb squad had to be alerted and this meant the work progressed in fits and starts, but eventually the problem was cleared.

At the other end of the Valley the proposed airport moved a step closer to reality with the appointment of Bruce Unsted, former Deputy Director of London City Airport. Mr Unsted's role was to bring the scheme forward as a viable enterprise, but already doubts were growing as to whether or not the airport would be ready for opening in 1993 as originally intended. The problem was the recession—still far from over—and the unwillingness of airlines to commit to any kind of schedule for flights in and out of Sheffield.

If the large-scale airport project was threatening to stall, the same could not be said of a much smaller, but equally interesting development by the River Don. This was the creation of

Figure 55. An excavator sits at the bottom of a concrete trench giving some sense of scale as the old steelworks' foundations are dug out of the Atlas North site.

the Five Weirs Walk, a five-mile footpath and cycleway running from Meadowhall to the city and taking in along the way much of the Valley's industrial heritage as well as some surprisingly attractive locations.

It was at one of these—the mill race at Sanderson's Weir—that artist David Nash unveiled his latest outdoor sculpture, the *Eye of the Needle and Sweeping Birches*. Nash planted 200 young silver birches in a sweeping arc designed to grow up around the central piece: a 30 foot high charred, split oak cut into the shape of a huge needle. The viewing point was a ten-tonne block of steel formerly used as a furnace plug. People either liked it or loathed it, but there was no mistaking that the sculpture marked the start of significant changes for the better along the riverside, and soon hundreds of people were walking along the finished sections of the footpath and enjoying the sight of rare plants and hosts of butterflies and moths that circled and wheeled over the much cleaner waters of the Don.

Figure 56. The head office of Thomas Jessop & Co.—a ghostly reminder of vanished glory.

One landmark, however, disappeared in 1992. This was the old head office of Thomas Jessop and Co. whose works once covered 30 acres in Brightside. Closed in 1980, the building had been steadily deteriorating since that time and was suffering from serious structural damage—the old concrete beams that held it up were literally rotting away.

Too expensive to restore, but of great historic and architectural value, the building was briefly the focus of intense debate within the SDC as ways were sought to preserve it, but at the end of the day it proved impossible to find a solution. The demolition teams moved in, and sadly, another part of the traditional East End vanished to make way for new jobs in new businesses.

In July 1992 the government finally dismissed a public inquiry appeal into the Development Corporation's compulsory purchase plans. By then the old controversy had fizzled out and the proceedings attracted little attention. Though it now had the official power to buy up companies, the SDC had already reduced its programme considerably and needed to relocate just 22 firms—a far cry from the 150 first threatened by the CPO programme. Schemes were being put in place to make sure that companies

Figure 57. New, functional buildings were designed for companies who were relocated by the SDC because of the new road scheme.

who elected to move premises could do so and still remain in business, with the prospect of working out of much better modern buildings at the end of the day.

The good news was tempered by the effects of the recession which was still dragging on. SDC Chairman Hugh Sykes acknowledged the way this was putting the brakes on regeneration when he said, 'The current business climate is exceptionally difficult, competition with other cities is fierce'. Chief Executive Graham Kendall also added this warning: 'Developments are taking longer to secure, which means we will not have completed the regeneration we were forecasting by 1995, when we are due to come to an end'.

It was a salutary reminder that the life of the Development Corporation was finite. But even though things looked bleak for the two big schemes of the airport and the canal basin regeneration, the SDC seemed to be recovering its confidence at the start of 1993 and was taking a new, tough stance towards developers who would not or could not progress schemes.

So it was that the Development Corporation felt strong enough to remain committed to the airport project when A.F. Budge went into liquidation in the new year. It also took back responsibility for the canal basin scheme when Norwest Holst failed to progress it within the expected timescales. The project was split up into smaller, more manageable schemes and put on the market again, with the added impetus of a promise from the SDC to spend money on the key historic listed buildings at the heart of the site, plus infrastructure work including road improvements, landscaping and the construction of a multi-storey car park.

This confidence was rewarded in April when the government announced that the SDC was to receive an extension of life. The extra time would take it through to the end of March 1997, and there was going to be a further £10 million grant to swell the Corporation's budget. This was a clear indication that the SDC was viewed in a positive light and that success was finally within its grasp.

Now things began to move. Local developers J.F. Finnegan signed a deal to build a series of speculative units on the Atlas South site. This agreement saw an initial 20,000-square-foot unit erected and then snapped up by Bridisco, a major distributor of gas and electrical appliances. More companies moved on to the Atlas North site, following in the footsteps of George Banks. These included Orion Insulations, Torch Telecom, abrasives specialists Abercon, Slater Printing and a unique UK/Korean joint venture: Davy Distington. The latter represented a major breakthrough for Sheffield as one of its largest and most respected engineering companies, Davy McKee struck a deal with Korea's giant steel company POSCO to design sophisticated steelworks that would operate around the world, manufacturing steel strip by continuous casting processes that could do away with the need for expensive rolling mills.

The Don Valley Link Road took shape. Its impact on the Valley was tremendous and it seemed to stimulate firms along its length to improve their premises with the help of money from the Development Corporation as well as activating key sites that had lain dormant for many years.

Figure 58. Keeping the Valley on the move: the Don Valley Link Road was the single largest project undertaken by the SDC.

The road had undergone many design revisions before work actually started on it. In the event, it proved possible to make it a four-lane highway for much of its length, although ambitious plans for landscaping along its central reservation had to be scaled down. This, however, was a minor point compared to the dramatic effect the road had on the appearance of the area. As old walls were removed and the final derelict factories came down, views were opened up that had been hidden for up to a century. Gone were the old, claustrophobic corridors between black industrial sheds. The far sides of the Valley could clearly be seen and a much cleaner, brighter picture was revealed.

This new sense of space was used to good effect by the Development Corporation which introduced some carefully planned landscaping at key points. For one scheme at Carbrook Hall, the SDC went back to the formal orchards of the eighteenth and early nineteenth century and planted pear and lime trees around the listed Carbrook Hall public house and the new Abbey National building. The addition of large areas of greenery dramatically relieved the industrial and commercial landscape. Suddenly people started to see the reality of the new-look Valley and understand that it was now much more than some attractive ideas on paper.

Figure 59. Lime trees and new offices transformed the Carbrook area.

The road continued through Carbrook and turned right opposite the Sheffield Arena to cross over the River Don at the old Abyssinia bridge. Emerging opposite Sheffield Forgemasters at the junction of Hawke Street and Brightside Lane, the road incorporated a new roundabout which had, by way of a reminder of what the Valley was famous for, a huge one-piece casting placed in its centre like a strange modern sculpture. The oddly shaped metal was, in fact, part of the leg of an ocean drilling platform and represented the application of some very sophisticated Sheffield technology, but some people thought it was supposed to be a work of art and complained about it to the papers.

There was no mistaking the purpose of the road, however. It thrust towards the city centre, running straight as an arrow down Brightside Lane parallel with the River Don. For the curious, turning left onto the reclaimed Newhall site, a footpath led down to the waterside where an odd, gnarled tree pushed its head above the railings. Close inspection during the spring and early summer would reveal the small, unripe fruits growing on its branches. This was one of the famous fig trees which germinated along the Don when the river ran warm and steaming during the height of Sheffield's industrial glory days. As this was long before the time of interceptor sewers, the fig stones had been washed down into the fertile silt of the river banks in Victorian effluent before taking hold and providing the city's East End with a tiny glimpse of Mediterranean summers in the oddest of locations.

The road continued under a British Rail bridge before splitting into two one-way sections along Savile Street East. Motorists heading into town were taken behind a block of factories including the site where engineers Hattersley and Davidson had added an unusual business to their portfolio: the manufacture of ice skating blades, worn by a large proportion of the best figure skaters in the world.

Emerging to join up with its other leg just before the old Albion Works of Thos. W. Ward, the road then ran to the Wicker Arch—part of the long complex of viaducts and archways that used to feed goods and passengers to and from Sheffield's Victoria station and the canal basin.

The significance of the road project—the biggest single item of expenditure by the Development Corporation—can today be seen in the form of new companies and new jobs created on the sites along its length. These sites include Abyssinia, where Whitbread opened a new hotel, and mail order specialists Freemans announced plans to build an ultra-modern call centre: exactly the kind of business that Sheffield's rival Leeds had been winning up to then, and a major step forward for the service sector within the steel city.

It came as a shock to some people that Sheffield could compete so well on the office front, but the Development Corporation recognized the advantages inherent in the Lower Don Valley when it came to schemes like these, namely: ease of parking, quick access from the motorway or city centre, attractive sites, purpose-built premises and an excellent potential workforce on the doorstep.

Because of these advantages, places like the Carbrook Hall Business Park filled up rapidly, with new office buildings constructed by Hallamshire Investments and Business Homes. Similar projects proved very successful at Meadowcourt, adjacent to junction 34 on the M1, while the old Spear and Jackson Aetna site on Savile Street East was taken by motor dealers Dixon's for a large scheme.

The SDC actively marketed the Valley to tap into the changing perceptions of customers. This was the first time that anyone had ever taken such an approach with the area—a concept well beyond the reach of even the most zealous Victorian reformer and certainly one that would have drawn blank looks from those great, early industrialists. But the proof was there in front of everyone's eyes: the area could be significantly changed by application of a great deal of effort and a relatively large amount of money, properly targeted and controlled.

Everywhere people went in the Lower Don Valley, the evidence could be seen that the Development Corporation was making a difference.

Newhall, a 20 acre industrial site attracted companies including spray nozzle manufacturers Lechler and Swedish-owned Standard Piston Rings. Welding equipment specialists Lincoln Electric took on the refurbishment of a large industrial shed at Southside, while their neighbours Gripple Ltd. restored the historic West Gun Works to make a brilliantly simple, yet effective wire joiner that had already won the Prince of Wales Award for Innovation and had become a runaway success in world markets.

Success followed success at the canal basin, now renamed Victoria Quays. The Straddle warehouse was beautifully refurbished by British Waterways who also renovated the canal and built a new Basin Manager's office on the quayside. New

Figure 60. Gripple Managing Director Hugh Facey smiles as he holds up his world-beating products against the backdrop of renovation that transformed the West Gun Works into a showpiece factory (copyright John Houlihan).

offices scheduled to be constructed overlooking the basin were snapped up by legal firm Nabarro Nathanson and turned into a northern headquarters specializing in law for industry. The promised car park was built by Henry Boot and even more offices added on the old Furnival Yard site, alongside a site for a new four star Stakis hotel, scheduled for completion in spring 1997.

What had changed? Certainly the SDC's approach to the regeneration of this particular scheme. Rather than rely on the actions of large developers who were very susceptible to the vagaries of economics and the whims of the market, it had instead relied on its own abilities to control and shape projects, drawing up a master plan that delivered steady progress. The idea was simple: pledge money to refurbish the historic buildings— that would immediately remove a financial burden from developers. Show you mean business when it comes to building roads and putting in new landscaping—then customers would know they would not be moving into a half-finished site. Get the central part finished and looking good—that would help sell the rest of the scheme.

Figure 61. Something to fly the flags for. The beautifully restored Victoria Quays development.

So successful was the Victoria Quays project that the SDC felt confident enough to ask the Prince of Wales to officially launch it in the winter of 1994. Never one to mince his words when it came to delivering a frank opinion on development schemes, the Prince was full of praise for the work of the Development Corporation which he saw from a unique perspective as a passenger on the first canal boat to exit the Terminal Warehouse since the 1970s.

In May the following year the SDC were far enough advanced with the project to open up the Quays to the Sheffield public in a three-day festival that drew some 60,000 people to the site. A host of performers including jazz musicians and circus artists added vibrancy and colour to the basin, set against the backdrop of more than three hundred beautiful canal boats that had converged on the Quays from all over the UK.

Figure 62. Festival time at Victoria Quays as 60,000 people flock to its public opening.

Figure 63. (Right) History preserved: the listed Siemens arch was dismantled, cleaned and moved down the road to complement the new buildings on President Park.

Figure 64. (Left) The renovated Sheaf Works at Victoria Quays, now a Tom Cobbleigh pub.

The high point of the event was an evening spectacular that saw the waters of the canal come alive in a display of dancing fountains lit by flickering laser light, set against a backdrop of fireworks and rousing music. Nothing like it had ever been seen in Sheffield before, said the papers, and for the SDC it was an immensely satisfying experience to see so many people taken up in the excitement and optimism of the show.

There was a commercial spin-off as well. The publicity that the event attracted further boosted the interest being shown in Victoria Quays by developers and potential occupiers of buildings. By the end of the year, the lovely old Wharf Street buildings at the front of the site had been sensitively restored and were home to the Monaghan Partnership, and the Straddle Warehouse was rumoured to have attracted the interest of a substantial professional services company. At the other end of the site, the old Sheaf Works—the first steam-powered cutlery factory in the city—was snapped up for leisure development and assured of a future as a beautifully restored centerpiece, attracting visitors down the length of the basin and providing much sought-after amenities for the new workers who would be based in the offices on the quayside.

If the drive through the heart of the Valley in 1995 had become an encouraging trip for everyone concerned with the city's future, 1996 proved even more heartening.

A tower crane rearing up above the city skyline marked where the Stakis hotel was taking shape on Victoria Quays, and where a new access road to the site off the Sheffield Parkway was being completed, running down past the old Sheaf Works, now sensitively restored and transformed into a Tom Cobbley leisure pub. Nabarro Nathanson had occupied their buildings and were already talking of expansion, growing their Sheffield operation to 230 people.

Figure 65. The new premises of Three Star Engineering have transformed the view across the 20 acre President Park site.

Dixon's motor city on the Aetna site had opened, creating 300 jobs. On President Park opposite, large areas of land were snapped up by engineering companies, including a specialized fastenings manufacturer. Soon the old steam hammer on the corner of the site would have a backdrop of new buildings and landscaping to contrast with its stark, powerful lines.

Meadowcourt continued to expand with phase three proving just as attractive and successful as the preceding two had been. More offices were planned at the back of Meadowhall, overlooking the River Don.

Attercliffe was finally getting its long-standing special development pro-gramme activated, with £1 million of SDC cash pumped into traffic calm-ing, road repairs and building refurbishment, plus a further £2 million earmarked to encourage more businesses into the centre. The Banner's department store—the Meadowhall of its day—had already been given a

Figure 66. Symbol of a new Attercliffe. The refurbished Adelphi cinema is once again a leisure magnet for local people.

new lease of life as a themed centre featuring Sheffield during the Blitz, along with selling space for antiques and associated memorabilia; now other premises would follow, revitalizing the old heart of the Valley.

The airport—much delayed, much debated (and much needed by local businesses) became a reality under the guidance of the SDC and developers Glenlivet. The first flights were scheduled for December 1996, with the airport designed to start small, anticipating a moderate amount of business in its first few years and then growing in a modular fashion, adding facilities and capacity until the market demand for larger aircraft kicked in. Interestingly, the emphasis was again on practicality—making the scheme a working, visible reality and then building on its success rather than going all-out for one expensive and ultimately risky project.

Figure 67. The runway at Sheffield Airport.

Back to the ground, and tool manufacturer James Neil made a significant announcement that it would set up operations on the Atlas North site, involving some 400 jobs. Specialist stationery company Santoro Graphics followed suit, as did Stainless Plating and Gleason's on Newhall. Steelwork for the Freemans call centre—designed to house 800 jobs—started to spring up opposite the Sheffield Arena, while on the far side of Broughton Lane the race was on to see if leisure giants THI could get a huge cinema, restaurant and entertainment complex up and running before Meadowhall completed its own expansion scheme involving a similar multi-screen complex. Encouraged by this localized boom, the City Council also entered the fray with plans for converting the old Carbrook school and putting together yet another leisure package.

Exciting times, and a situation that was guaranteed to generate controversy right to the end of the SDC's life. However, anyone who really examined the big issues, the long-running themes and important strands made up of decisions, actions and physical changes, came to identical conclusions: the Valley had been transformed, almost beyond recognition, by dint of single-mindedness, the intelligent application of resources and a partnership approach to the fundamentals of regeneration.

Where there had been dependence on one industry, there was now diversity, with companies specializing in continuous casting, cutlery, fastenings and welding rubbing shoulders with those carrying out printing, food processing, electrical engineering, financial services, software production and packaging—to name only a few of the sectors represented.

Where there had been dereliction there were new buildings and there were new jobs, bringing confidence and hope to Sheffield. A crumbling infrastructure had been replaced by modern roads, a ragged environment had been improved, managed and shaped to give pleasure to workers and visitors alike. The best of the past had been preserved and blended sensitively with the best of the present.

The timescale for change, in relation to the long history of the Valley, had been remarkably short. A blink of an eye really; a moment as fleeting as the spark from a furnace during which a huge drama of destruction and rebirth was played out across the 2000 acres of Sheffield's East End.

The SDC has finished its work. At the time of writing, the organization was winding up operations and the team was dispersing as people took new jobs and tackled new challenges.

But still the story goes on. Other people, other organizations will feature now, and in twenty, fifty, a hundred years time, other histories will be written charting future successes and failures, the hopes and triumphs of later generations, their good times mixed with the bad.

It is to be hoped that there are more of the former than the latter. The Valley deserves to grow and prosper—the spirit of the workers and the industrial leaders who made it great can still be found there, their standards of quality and dedication to craftsmanship live on. Every product—even the smallest item—that leaves the factories and workshops continues their proud tradition and says to the world, 'This was made in Sheffield'.

Long may it be so.

Conclusion: A Future for the Valley

The story of the Lower Don Valley does not, of course, end with the demise of the Sheffield Development Corporation. Some important projects that have been initiated by the Corporation are still under construction. In the year after the SDC is wound up many new offices, industrial buildings, leisure complexes and hotels will be opened, all bringing more jobs to the Valley.

The shape of the Valley in the immediate future is clear. It is a busy, confident mixed economy which should succeed whatever the vagaries of the general economic climate. All the building blocks are in place and through difficult times Valley companies have learnt to compete in world markets.

This new and exciting environment will encourage new companies to join those who have decided to invest there. More companies in industries new to the Valley, such as Abbey National, Freemans, Halifax Building Society and Nabarro Nathanson, will choose to locate there.

To a very considerable extent the Lower Don Valley's future is linked to that of the City of Sheffield as a whole. The successful regeneration of the area has brought with it a new spirit of partnership in the City and a new confidence in the future. Both the Valley and the City are now much stronger and more able to attract the employment that is so necessary to generate the wealth required to improve the quality of life of its citizens.

This book has traced some 2500 years of history and its theme has been change, both planned and unplanned. The only certain thing about the future is that change will continue. The hope is that it will be of the positive, planned kind of the last eight and a half years of the Valley's history. In handing over the baton to other partners in the city we wish them well with the continuing regeneration process.

Hugh Sykes, DL

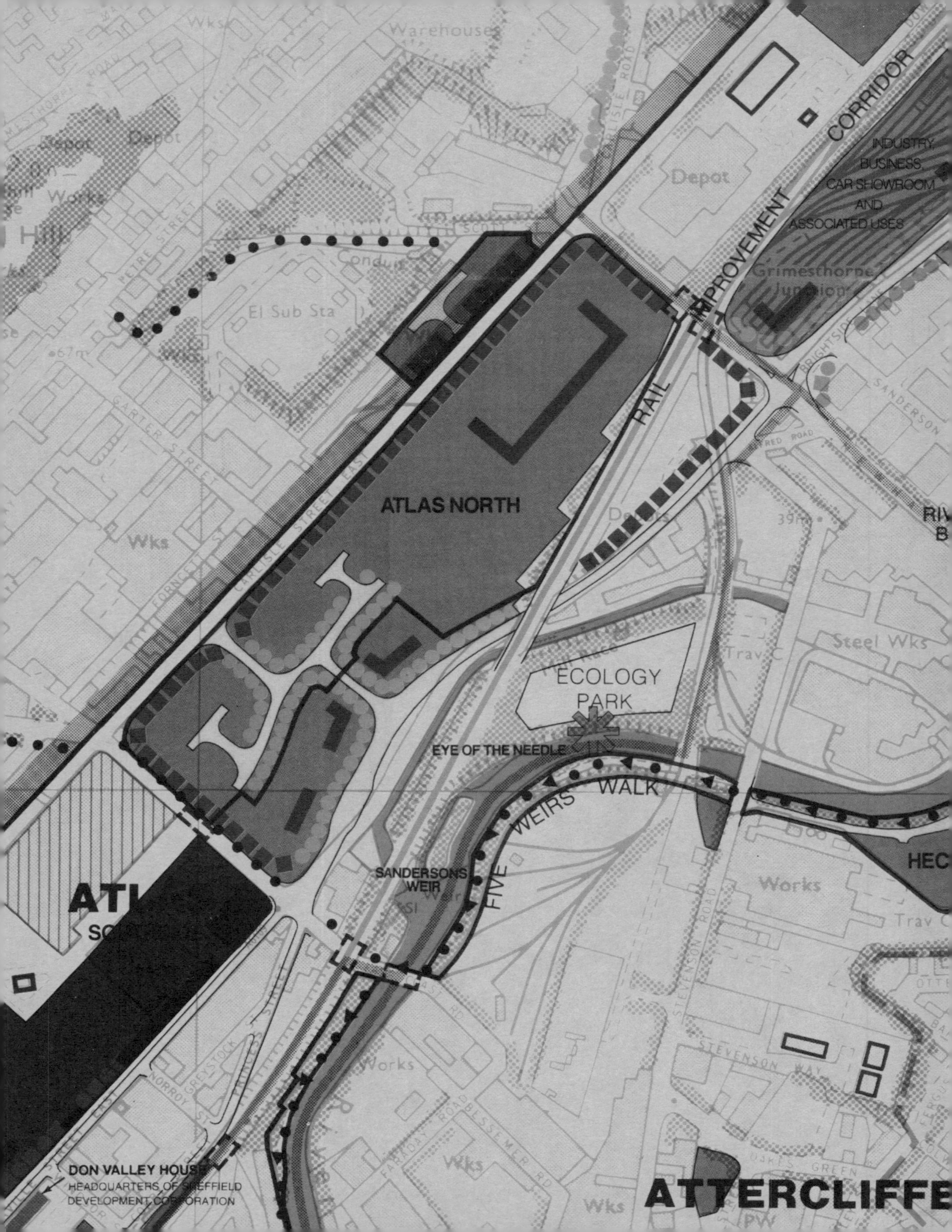

CORRIDOR

INDUSTRY
BUSINESS,
CAR SHOWROOM
AND
ASSOCIATED USES

Depot

Grimesthorne
Junction

RAIL

ATLAS NORTH

ECOLOGY
PARK

EYE OF THE NEEDLE

WALK

WEIRS

SANDERSONS
WEIR

FIVE

ATI
SC

HEC

Works

Trav

DON VALLEY HOUSE
HEADQUARTERS OF SHEFFIELD
DEVELOPMENT CORPORATION

ATTERCLIFFE

Wks